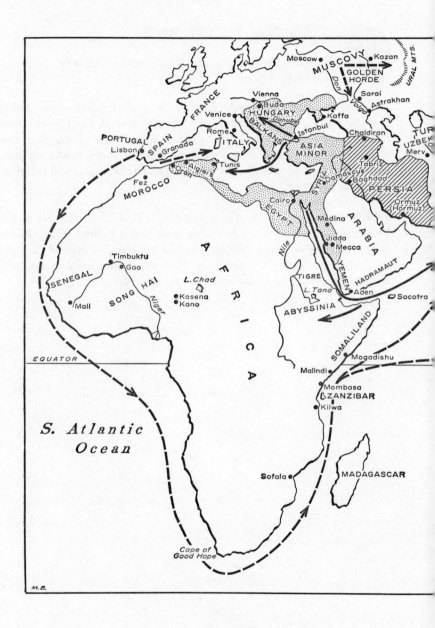

THE GLOBAL HISTORY SERIES

Leften Stavrianos, *Northwestern University*

General Editor

This series aims to present history in global perspective, going beyond national or regional limitations, and dealing with over-riding trends and forces. The various collections of original materials span the globe, range from prehistoric times to the present, and include anthropology, economics, political science, and religion, as well as history.

John J. Saunders, editor of this volume, is Reader in History at the University of Canterbury, New Zealand, and a Fellow of the Royal Asiatic Society of Great Britain. He has written *The Age of Revolution, Aspects of the Crusades, A History of Medieval Islam,* and numerous articles on Islam and Eastern history.

THE MUSLIM WORLD
C. 1530 A.D.

STAN
FARGHANA
Jaxortes
Samarkand
HINDU KUSH
Indus
MOGULS
Panipat
Delhi
Ganges
Daibul
UJARAT
Diu
Cambay
INDIA
MALABAR
VIJAYANAGAR
Goa
Calicut
Pulicat
CEYLON

KANSUH

CHINA

Pacific Ocean

PHILIPPINE
ISLANDS

Kelantan
ACHEH
SUMATRA
Malacca
BORNEO
MOLUCCAS
(Spice Is.)
CELEBES
Bantam
JAVA
Macassar

Indian Ocean

AUSTRALIA

Ottoman Empire

Safavid Persia

Mogul India

Muslim "drives" against
Christendom

Christian "drives" against
Islam

THE MUSLIM WORLD ON THE EVE
OF EUROPE'S EXPANSION

EDITED BY JOHN J. SAUNDERS

A SPECTRUM BOOK

Prentice-Hall, Inc. / *Englewood Cliffs, N.J.*

FOR

PHILIP AND MARION

CONTENTS

THE MUSLIM WORLD ON THE EVE

OF EUROPE'S EXPANSION

GENERAL INTRODUCTION

The century from 1450 to 1550 was a decisive one in the agelong struggle between Islam and Christendom. In 1450 the Muslim offensive against Europe was being pressed with vigor by the Ottoman Turks; Constantinople was about to fall, the Balkan peninsula was being overrun, and the Christian Powers were fighting desperately to hold the line of the Danube. The Muslims, proud of their rich and ancient culture, did not doubt their superiority in every field over their Christian foes. Nearly all the great highways of international trade were in Muslim hands, and the wealth of the Muslim kingdoms was drawn largely from the profits of commerce. By 1550 the situation had been almost magically transformed. Though Hungary had fallen in 1526, Vienna had repulsed a Turkish attack, and the Ottoman advance ground to a halt in face of the resistance of the Austrian and Spanish Hapsburgs on the Middle Danube and on the Mediterranean. A bitter religious quarrel between Turkey and Persia sapped the strength of both Powers. The Renaissance was lifting the cultural level of Western Europe well above that of the Muslim East. The Portuguese, by finding a way to India via the Cape, had broken the Arab trade monopoly of the Indian Ocean, damaged the economy of the Muslim states, and exposed the Islamic world to assault from the sea. Only in northern India, where the brilliant adventurer Babur had founded the Mogul empire in 1526, did Islam seem to face a promising future.

The Ottoman Empire was the greatest Muslim Power of this age, and seemed destined at one time to bring almost all the lands of Islam under its sway. Beginning as a small clan in the northwest

1

corner of Asia Minor around 1300, the Ottomans, or Osmanlis, had been cast for the role of *ghazis*, fighters for the faith in the perennial holy war against Christendom, represented for them by the decaying Byzantine Empire and the quarreling kingdoms and principalities of the Balkans. They were tough frontiersmen, whose geographical position made the Orthodox Christian lands of southeast Europe their obvious field of expansion. Their sultans, to stiffen their civil and military establishments with men who were free from tribal and other loyalties and on whose fidelity they could depend, developed about 1400 the peculiar institution known as the *devshirme*, periodical levies of boys from the conquered Christian Balkan countries, who were taken from their families, educated in the Muslim faith, and trained as soldiers or administrators. These non-Turks formed the core of the Janissaries ("new troops"), crack regiments of infantry, whose discipline, arms, and equipment were for long superior to anything the Christian Powers could show.

Under Muhammad, or Mehmet, the Conqueror (1451-81), Constantinople was taken and the Byzantine Empire snuffed out, the Danube was passed, Trebizond, the last Christian state on the mainland of Asia, captured, and Italy invaded. The fall of Constantinople in 1453 gave the Ottomans an impregnable capital and an unrivaled military and naval base and earned them the respect of all Islam, for the taking of Constantine's city had been a goal of Muslim endeavor since the days of the Prophet himself. The threat to Western Europe was grave. If Italy were conquered and Rome went the way of Constantinople, the Ottoman armies might not be stopped by the Alps or the Pyrenees. The Popes strove desperately to organize a new crusade and induce the Western kingdoms to drop their quarrels and unite against the Turkish menace.

In fact, Europe was saved by quite unexpected developments, which caused the Turkish offensive against the West to be virtually suspended for forty years (1481-1520). First, the Conqueror's son and successor Bayezid II (1481-1512), styled *Veli* ("the Saint"), was a quiet and unwarlike prince, devoted to religion and the arts. Secondly, his brother Jem, defeated in an attempt to seize the throne, fled to the West and was held as a hostage for thirteen years (1482-95); the Sultan was thus obliged to be circumspect in his dealings with the Christian states while this dangerous personage was alive and in their hands. Thirdly, the sudden emergence in Persia in 1500 of the Safavid regime, whose leader Isma'il was in the eyes of most Muslims, including the Turks, a blasphemous heretic, obliged the Ottoman government to switch its attention to its eastern frontier. Fears began to grow in Constantinople that Isma'il might ally himself with the Mamluks of Egypt, and in 1512 the aged and pacific Bayezid was deposed in favor of his ruthless and energetic son Selim the Grim (1512-20), who lost no time in striking out at these dangers with all the force at his command. His armies invaded Persia and routed Isma'il at Chaldiran in Azerbaijan (1514), then turning south, smashed through the Mamluk defenses of Syria and Egypt and occupied Cairo (1517). The old Arabic-speaking heartlands of Islam were thereby annexed to the Ottoman Empire, and the sultan's power was extended to Arabia and the Red Sea. Not until the accession of Sulaiman in 1520 was the war in the West seriously resumed, Rhodes taken (1522), Hungary conquered (1526), and Vienna besieged (1529).

It was during this forty years' breathing space that Europe was able to gain a series of substantial advantages in widely separated regions. In 1480, just before the death of Muhammad II, Ivan III of Russia, with the support of the rival khanate of the Crimea, beat back the last attempt of the Turco-Mongol Golden Horde—which had been encamped on the lower Volga since the days of Chingiz (Jenghiz) Khan—to enforce the old tribute payment. The Ottomans had gained a footing in the Crimea in 1475, and they forced the Krim Tatar khanate into vassalage; but they were too late to save the Horde, which disintegrated and disappeared in 1502. Its destruction was a blow to Islam in Eastern Europe and cleared the path for Russian expansion beyond the Volga and the Urals into Asia. At the other end of Europe, Granada, the last stronghold of the Moors in Spain, fell in 1492 to the armies of Ferdinand and Isabella, whose marriage in 1479 had united the kingdoms of Castile and Aragon. Bayezid, responding to a doleful plea from the Moorish sovereign, had for the first time dispatched an Ottoman fleet into the western Mediterranean, but it accomplished little and failed to rescue the last remnant of Spanish Islam. Nor could it stop the Spaniards from carrying the war into Africa and seizing in quick succession a number of Barbary ports and the rocky islet of the

Peñon commanding the harbor of Algiers. And in 1498 Vasco da Gama, having successfully rounded the Cape, appeared off Calicut in south India, and a new phase in the history of the world began. The Indian Ocean had been for centuries an Arab lake. Occasionally, Chinese trading fleets were seen there, but they seem to have disappeared after 1440. Arab commercial colonies were strung out along the coast of East Africa as far south as Mozambique; Arab ships were regular callers at the ports of Ceylon and the Malabar coasts; Arab merchants had turned Malacca into a big international *entrepôt*; and these same traders were carrying the faith of Islam into Malaya, Indonesia, and the Philippines. The chronology of the conversion of Southeast Asia to Islam is uncertain, but the fall of the Hindu kingdom of Majapahit in eastern Java in 1478, or a little later, undoubtedly gave a big advantage to the Muslims, and by 1500 paganism and Hinduism in these lands were in retreat. The silks and spices and precious stones of the Far East were carried in Arab vessels up the Persian Gulf and the Red Sea; the cargoes were mostly discharged in Egypt to the great profit of its rulers, who allowed Venetians and other Westerners to purchase their share for shipment to Europe.

Egypt had been governed since 1250 by the Mamluks, a military caste of ex-slaves originally purchased from the Turkish-speaking tribes of south Russia and the Caucasus. The regime was a kind of permanent military dictatorship; the Mamluk sultan was chosen by the amirs, or generals, hereditary succession was rare, and the throne was often a prize to be snatched by ambitious officers. The Mamluks were proudly race conscious and despised the native Egyptians; they oppressed the peasants and exploited the townsmen; and the conservatism of these arrogant mounted warriors disdained the regular employment of new-fangled firearms and artillery, which the Ottoman had used to good effect at the capture of Constantinople. They had some pretensions to culture: They were great builders and patrons of Arabic scholarship and letters, which had found a refuge in Egypt when Baghdad was sacked by the Mongols in 1258. The prosperity of Egypt was bound up with continued Arab control of the Indian Ocean; when this broke down, the Mamluks faced economic ruin and growing unpopularity and were easily swept away by the Ottoman invasion of 1516-17.

The Portuguese entry into the Indian Ocean threw the Muslim kingdoms into alarm and confusion. Fleet after fleet sailed from Lisbon round the Cape in the wake of da Gama, and the great viceroys, Almeida and Albuquerque, used this naval power to set up a string of bases all round the shores of this vast sea. Sofala, Kilwa, and Mombasa in East Africa were taken in 1505, the island of Socotra in 1507, and Malacca in 1511. "So hunted was Arab shipping that even the coastal craft had to steal from creek to creek." [1] Asian trade was diverted to Lisbon; in 1507 no Indian wares of any kind reached Egypt. Seriously disturbed, the Mamluks fitted out a fleet to challenge these audacious intruders and sent it down the Red Sea to western India, but it was soundly beaten off Diu in 1509. In 1513, however, the Portuguese met their first check: They failed in an attempt on Aden, the capture of which would have enabled them to close the Red Sea to Muslim shipping and threaten the holy cities of Mecca and Medina. The Mamluks sent an expeditionary force to the Yemen in 1515, probably hoping to use this corner of Arabia as a base for an anti-Portuguese offensive, but the only effect was to weaken their strength at home at the very moment that they had to meet attack from the Ottomans. A single campaign by Selim in 1516-17 sufficed to overthrow the Mamluk regime, which died unregretted.

The Ottomans were aware that, by taking possession of Egypt, they were assuming the defense of Islam against the seapower of Spain in the Mediterranean and of Portugal in the Indian Ocean. In Cairo, Selim was shown a map of America, copied from one captured from a Spanish ship, and in 1519 he appointed, as beylerbey of Algiers, the great corsair Khair ad-Din Barbarossa, who had long been striving to halt the progress of Spain along the Barbary coast. Ottoman power now reached into the western Mediterranean, but not as far as the Straits of Gibraltar, control of which might have allowed the Turks to cut the communications of Spain and Portugal with America and the East. Not long after the Ottoman conquest of Egypt, a new front in the war between Islam and Christendom was opened up in Abyssinia. That ancient Christian kingdom was menaced by a Muslim Somali invasion led by one

[1] R. B. Serjeant, *The Portuguese off the South Arabian Coasts*, Oxford, 1963, p. 14.

Ahmad Gran, who received help from the Turks; for a time it seemed that the Islamic tide would sweep over the whole country, but the assault was beaten off by 1543 with assistance from the ubiquitous Portuguese. Meanwhile Sultan Sulaiman had conquered Iraq in 1536 and pushed the Ottoman frontier to the Persian Gulf; the naval war with Portugal was vigorously pressed, but with no better success than the Mamluks had had. A great Turco-Egyptian armada was routed, again off Diu, in 1538, and by the 1550s the attempt to break the power of Portugal in Indian waters was tacitly abandoned, with disastrous consequences to the Muslim world. Well might the Turks ruefully say, "God has given the land to us but the sea to the Christians!"

This failure was closely associated with the situation in Persia. The clash between Ottoman and Safavids was fatal to Islam's chances of successfully meeting the European challenge on the seas. This was no mere national rivalry, but a bitter theological quarrel. Shah Isma'il (1500-1524) claimed descent from Ali and imposed on his people the doctrines of the Shi'a, the party that rated Ali and the Imams as the infallible mouthpieces of God—a belief condemned as a vicious heresy by the rest of the Muslim world. Venerated by his followers as the living emanation of God, Isma'il was far more than a king, and his government, almost a pure theocracy. Constantinople was gravely alarmed. The Turcoman tribes of Anatolia and the Bektash order of dervishes, which was strongly rooted in the same region, were already deeply infected with Shi'ite ideas, and the rise of the new Shi'ite regime in Persia was bound to exert a powerful pull on them and endanger the stability of the Ottoman Empire. Sultan Selim resolved on drastic measures. In 1514 all known or suspected Shi'ites in his dominions were rounded up and imprisoned or executed, the orthodox Muslim doctors of the law having pronounced it more meritorious to kill one Shi'ite heretic than seventy Christian unbelievers. (Forty thousand are said to have perished; it was worse than St. Bartholomew's Day in Paris in 1572.) Selim then invaded Persia, routed the Safavid army at Chaldiran, and captured Isma'il's capital, Tabriz. His hopes of completely destroying Isma'il's power were, however, ruined by unrest verging on mutiny in his own forces. The *ghazis* held it was no business of theirs to fight fellow Muslims, and the Janissaries had close links with the

Bektash dervishes. Selim was compelled to retire from Persia; the Safavids were saved, the schism in the world of Islam became permanent, and the Persians sought alliance with the Western Powers against the Turks, whose dream of restoring the old universal Muslim empire of the caliphs was dissipated forever.

The Safavid schism had wide repercussions. It thrust a Shi'ite wedge into the heart of Sunnite Islam and cut off the Ottomans from their fellow orthodox in the East. It also contributed indirectly to the establishment of the Mogul empire in India, whose founder Babur was once a protégé of Shah Isma'il's. Babur, a prince of mixed Turkish and Mongol blood, who inherited the small kingdom of Farghana north of the Hindu Kush, found himself fighting alongside the Safavids against the Uzbeks, a tribal confederacy that rose to power in Central Asia after the fall of the Golden Horde. But his association with the heretics damaged his cause, the Uzbeks drove him from his homeland, and he betook himself to India, where the Muslim Sultanate of Delhi was breaking to pieces. By brilliant generalship and the skilful use of the new artillery, Babur won the battle of Panipat in 1526 and made himself master of the Gangetic plain. On this foundation his son Humayun (1530-56) and grandson Akbar (1556-1605) built up a formidable empire, Sunnite in faith but Persian in culture, which came in the end to rule nearly the whole Indian subcontinent. But it was essentially a land power, centered in the north, its expansion into the Deccan long blocked by the Hindu kingdom of Vijayanagar that survived till 1565; Babur in his famous *Memoirs* never once mentions the Portuguese, and no Mogul navy ever attempted to restore Muslim dominance over the Indian Ocean.

Thus, by the mid-sixteenth century Islam was dominated by three great land empires—Ottoman, Safavid, and Mogul—none of which was capable of driving the Europeans from the ocean highways and one of which was severed from the others by acute religious differences. Yet it would be a mistake to conclude that Islam was weak. It was still expanding on land. The Turkish danger was acutely felt in Europe; the Portuguese, however much they might have damaged Muslim trade, had made no real territorial inroads on Dar al-Islam and had indeed arrived in Malaya and the East Indies too late to stop the conversion of those lands to the faith of the

Prophet, though the Spaniards, by occupying the Philippines, probably checked the spread of Islam to Japan and coastal China.

The Muslim peoples, far from feeling any sense of inferiority, were convinced they had nothing whatever to learn from the barbarous Franks of the West, whom they still identified with the uncultured barons and knights of the Crusades. Of the vast stirrings of the European mind associated with the Renaissance, they knew nothing. No Western books were translated into Arabic, Persian, or Turkish; printing was despised as an infidel innovation, the Ottoman Empire doing without it till the early eighteenth century; while natural science was suspected as an impious prying into things with which the devout believer was not concerned. In these circumstances it is perhaps not surprising that Islam unconsciously fell behind the West in the intellectual race. Other factors were also involved. The old Arabic scholarship, long patronized by the Mamluks, decayed rapidly after the Ottoman conquest of Egypt; the Safavids, narrow and intense fanatics, discouraged secular learning and even poetry and *belleslettres;* whereas the Moguls, whose literature and architecture was of a high standard, were removed from the old centers of Islamic culture (Transoxiana being ruled by the semibarbarous Uzbeks) and so lacked the necessary stimulus to the cultivation of philosophy and science.

I / THE OTTOMAN EMPIRE

INTRODUCTION

"We raised a world-subduing Power from a tribe" was the boast of the Ottoman Turks, who in the early decades of the sixteenth century were masters of a vast imperial domain stretching from the frontiers of Austria to the Persian Gulf and from the Sahara to the Caucasus. A *ghazi* state dedicated to the advance of Islam, the Empire to its subjects *was* Islam, and indeed Safavid Persia and Mogul India were the only important Muslim kingdoms outside its control. Christendom had never been in greater peril since the time of the Arab conquests eight hundred years before, and, unlike the Arabs, the Turks had taken Constantinople and thrust deep into Europe as far as the gates of Vienna. During the reigns of the great warrior sultans, Selim I (1512-20) and Sulaiman the Magnificent (1520-66), the size of the Empire was doubled, and the Europeans, nervously apprehensive of this seemingly invincible enemy, sought to uncover the secrets of its success. The strange, unique institutions of Ottoman Turkey were scrutinized by a host of Western travelers, diplomats, publicists, and scholars, in consequence of which we are better informed about them than about those of any other Muslim land in this age.

1 / THE CHARACTER OF THE OTTOMAN EMPIRE

The nature of the Ottoman state has puzzled some observers and given rise to varying interpretations. By some it has been considered a successor state to Byzantium, by others a completely Oriental Islamic monarchy. Professor Bernard Lewis, a specialist in Turkish

9

*history and institutions, here shows how the character of the Empire
was transformed by Selim I's conquest of the Arabic-speaking lands
of the Middle East: From being a Muslim frontier state fighting
against the Christians of the Balkans, it changed into a mighty universal power, whose sovereign claimed the lordship of Islam and
dreamed of reviving the glories of the medieval caliphate.*

*In this they were following in the steps of their predecessors, the
Seljuk Turks, who entered Western Asia in the eleventh century
and seized most of Asia Minor from the Byzantines. As the latter
claimed to be the heirs of Rome, the Turks called them "Rumi"
(Romans); Asia Minor, "the land of Rum"; and the Seljuk princes
who reigned there, "sultans of Rum." These princes were the vassals
of the "Great Seljuks," who ruled in Persia and Iraq and claimed
to be sultans over all Islam. When the Seljuk power decayed and
disappeared, the Ottomans after an interval stepped into position,
first as sultans of Rum, that is, of the ex-Byzantine lands, and then,
after the conquests of Selim I and Sulaiman, sultans, or emperors,
of Islam.*

The Islamic tradition of politics and government came to the
Ottomans in a late and developed form, unified by many influences
and by long and painful experiences. Perhaps for that reason it was
able to serve them as an effective guide to the conduct of state, with
a set of rules of statecraft and government that were the practical
obverse side of its theory of rights and obligations.

It was to this complex heritage of state, statecraft and empire
that the Ottomans succeeded when they grew from border chieftains
into Muslim Sultans. Some have seen in Ottoman Istanbul a third,
Muslim Rome. Was "Sultan in Byzance," as Milton called him,
really the Emperor of a Turkish Rome—were his empire and his
institutions of government no more than the Byzantine Empire
with new names and outward forms? The theory at one time commanded some support, but has not stood up to critical examination.
The Byzantine Empire which the Ottomans encountered in the
fourteenth and fifteenth centuries was no longer the Empire of
Constantine, Justinian or even Heraclius. It was a pale and feeble
remnant of the past—and already half Westernized in its laws, its

government, even in its institutions of sovereignty. The final triumph of the Ottomans in 1453 laid the ghost of something that was already dead. . . . It was from the Sultan of Rum, rather than from any early or later emperor of Rome, that the Ottomans derived their theory and practice of government.

The most significant feature of the title Sultan of Rum is its connotation of a defined territorial sovereignty. The Great Seljuks had been Sultans of Islam—exercising the one and indivisible worldly power in the universal Muslim state. The Seljuks of Rum —and the Ottomans who revived their claims and titles—were Sultans of Rum, that is, of a definite country and people. The land of Rum was Anatolia, and for a time the Turks even called themselves Rumi, after the country they inhabited. The extension of the Ottoman State into Europe reinforced this claim; the lands of Rum—of the Byzantine Empire or rather of the Greek Orthodox Christendom —embraced territories in Europe as well as in Asia, and it was natural for the new masters of an important part of the estate to seek to acquire the whole of it. And so to the old land of Rum— Anatolia—was added the territory of Rumelia, both making up the patrimony of the Sultan of Rum.

In Ottoman writings of the fifteenth century the common title of their country is land of Rum, of their sovereign Sultan of Rum. This marks him off from his Muslim neighbours, the Sultans of Persia and Egypt, and expressed both the extent and the limits of his claims. The conquest of Constantinople was the completion rather than the initiation of a process of development.

Half a century later, the wars of Selim I against his Muslim neighbours, and the incorporation in the Ottoman Empire of the Arab lands in Asia and Africa, brought a reinforcement of the *Islamic* Imperial tradition.

The Empire was now no longer only that of Rum; it included the heartlands of Islam—the holy cities in Arabia, the seats of the great caliphs of Medina, Damascus, Baghdad and Cairo. The Sultan of Egypt had gone; the heretical Shah of Persia was extruded from the community of Sunni Islam—the Ottoman Sultan alone remained as the orthodox ruler of an Islamic state. True, there were still Sunni sovereigns in remote places like Morocco, Transoxiana and India, but these were too far away to make much impact. From

North Africa right across the Middle East there was now but one Sunni Islamic Sultan—and he ruled over all the realms of the Caliphs, save only for such as had been lost to infidels or heretics.

In the preamble to the *kanuns* (laws) of Suleyman the Magnificent (1520-66), the Sultan describes himself as "Sultan of the Arabs and Persians and Rum." Suleyman is thus claiming sovereignty over the three major peoples of classical Islam. The title "Sultan of Rum" is replaced by "Padishah-i Islam"—the Emperor of Islam. In this title, which is commonly used by Ottoman historians and others to describe the sovereign, the wheel has come full circle; territorial sovereignty is lost again in a simpler and vaster claim that makes the Ottoman Sultan what he indeed was—the heir to the great universal Empires of medieval Islam.

2 / THE OTTOMAN SLAVE SYSTEM: THE *DEVSHIRME*, OR CHILD TRIBUTE

The most startling feature of the Ottoman system of government and the one which shocked contemporary Europe was the devshirme, *the compulsory levy of Christian boys, who were taken from their families to be trained for posts in the civil or military establishment. This practice arose in the late fourteenth century. (The first clear reference to it dates from 1395.) It was probably designed to provide a reliable and disciplined force of infantry for siege work and garrison duty, since the* ghazi *cavalryman, the typical Turkish soldier of the early period, was a free and independent-minded warrior not amenable to control by the central government. The Christian lads pressed into Ottoman service were legally slaves; they were induced to turn Muslim, all ties of family, race, and religion were broken, and they were trained to absolute obedience to their new masters. Promotion was by merit, and such slaves could rise to the highest rank, becoming even grand vizier or commander in chief. The details of the actual levy are uncertain. It seems to have been made irregularly as the need arose; there were probably no fixed age limits, though boys in their teens were commonly chosen; orphans, only sons, and married youths were exempt; and the* devshirme *was rarely levied outside country districts. Strictly, the practice was contrary to Islamic law and violated the protection given to Christians living under Muslim rule. No trace of it is found in any other Muslim state. It has been suggested that some canonists*

*may have argued that people converted to Christianity after the
time of Muhammad were not entitled to this protection: This would
apply to almost all the Balkan nations except the Greeks. Professor
Lybyer here comments on what he calls "the Ottoman Ruling Institution."*

Perhaps no more daring experiment has been tried on a large
scale on the face of the earth than that embodied in the Ottoman
Ruling Institution. Its nearest ideal analogue is found in the Republic of Plato, its actual nearest parallel in the Mameluke system of
Egypt; but it was not restrained within the aristocratic Hellenic
limitations of the first, and it subdued and outlived the second.
. . . The Ottoman system deliberately took slaves and made them
ministers of state; it took boys from the sheep-run and the plow-
tail and made them courtiers and the husbands of princesses; it
took young men whose ancestors had borne the Christian name for
centuries and made them rulers in the greatest of Mohammedan
states, and soldiers and generals in invincible armies whose chief
joy was to beat down the Cross and elevate the Crescent. It never
asked its novices, "Who was your father?" or "What do you know?"
or even, "Can you speak our tongue?"; but it studied their faces
and their frames and said, "*You* shall be a soldier, and if you show
yourself worthy, a general," or, "*You* shall be a scholar and a
gentleman, and if the ability lies in you, a governor and a prime
minister." Grandly disregarding that fabric of fundamental customs
which is called "human nature," and those religious and social
prejudices which are thought to be almost as deep as life itself, the
Ottoman system took children forever from their parents, discouraged family cares among its members through their most active
years, allowed them no certain hold on property, gave them no
definite promise that their sons and daughters would profit by their
success and sacrifice, raised and lowered them with no regard for
ancestry or previous distinction, taught them a strange law, ethics
and religion, and even kept them conscious of a sword raised above
their heads which might put an end at any moment to a brilliant
career along a matchless path of human glory. . . .

From *The Government of the Ottoman Empire*, by A. H. Lybyer, pp. 45-46,
47-49. Copyright © 1913 by the Harvard University Press. Reprinted by permission of the publisher.

Every one who belonged to the Ruling Institution in any capacity from gardener to Grand Vizier, save only the members of the royal family, bore the title of *kul,* or slave, of the sultan. Nor was this title a mere form: with few exceptions, all members entered the system as actual slaves, and there was nowhere along the line of promotion any formal or real process of emancipation. The power of the sultan over the lives, persons and property of the members of the institution, and his right to their absolute obedience, bear every mark of having been derived from the idea of slavery. . . .

Four methods were employed for obtaining recruits for the system—. . . capture, purchase, gift, and tribute. Of these only the last is commonly considered; but it was originally, and probably always, merely supplementary to the others. The four methods ultimately rested on two. Slaves who were bought for the sultan or given to him had nearly all been either taken as captives or levied illegally with the tribute boys; there was hardly any other way, since slaves passed too rapidly into the Moslem fold to have their children available for the system. As to the comparative numbers obtained by the different methods, there are few data for calculation. Probably about three thousand tribute boys was the annual average in the sixteenth century . . . ; the whole number in the system may be estimated at about eighty thousand. Since the losses by war were sometimes tremendous, it is probable that the average annual renewal required was as much as one-tenth, or between seven and eight thousand. . . .

The levying was accomplished by a regular process, the *devshurmeh* (*devshirme*). Normally every four years, but oftener in case of need, a body of officials more skilled in judging boys than trained horse-dealers are in judging colts were sent out by the government to the regions from which tribute was taken. The whole of the Balkan Peninsula, Hungary, the western coast of Asia Minor, and the southern and eastern shores of the Black Sea were included in the territory visited; but the strongest and ablest youths came from the mountain regions inhabited by Albanians and the Southern Slavic peoples. The recruiting officers were commissioned each to bring in a certain number, which had been apportioned to them out of a total determined at the capital. There was no principle of tithing, and no fixed proportion or number of boys was levied from each village or family; the quota desired from each district was obtained for the government by selection of the most available youths. The recruiting officers sometimes collected a larger number than was asked for, and sold the surplus on their own account to high officials or wealthy private citizens. A regular procedure was followed. The officers obtained from the Christian priest of the village a list of the boys whom he had baptized, and who were between the ages of twelve and twenty years or thereabouts. All these were brought before the officers, who selected the best. Parents who had strong and well-favored sons might lose them all, while those who had weaklings would lose none. On leaving each village, the officer took with him the boys whom he had selected; and when his quota had been gathered, he took them to the capital.

3 / THE OTTOMAN ADMINISTRATION

The civil and military administration of the Ottoman Empire was for long the most efficient in Europe. Its principal features are delineated in the following extract from a study by an American scholar.

The Ottoman Empire sprawled over three continents. In Europe it included the Balkan Peninsula to the Danube River, together with the following provinces north of the river: Transylvania, Moldavia, Wallachia, most of Hungary, Podolia in Poland, and the entire north coast of the Black Sea. In Asia it included Asia Minor, Armenia, most of the Caucasus, the Tigris and Euphrates valleys down to the Persian Gulf, the western coast of the Persian Gulf, and all the lands on the eastern coast of the Mediterranean together with a wide strip running down the entire length of the Arabian Peninsula to the Gulf of Aden. Finally, in Africa, the empire encompassed Egypt, Tripoli, Tunis and Algiers. And to complete the picture we should add Crete, Cyprus, and the islands of the Aegean.

Within this vast empire lived peoples of diverse strains and creeds. The Turks, Tatars, Arabs, Kurds, Turkomans, Berbers and Mamelukes all belonged to Islam, together with large numbers of

From *The Balkans Since 1453*, by L. S. Stavrianos. Copyright © 1958 by L. S. Stavrianos. Used by permission of Holt, Rinehart and Winston, Inc., publishers. *All rights reserved.*

Bosnians, Albanians and Bulgarians who had apostatized to the conquering creed. The remaining ethnic groups—Greeks, Hungarians, South Slavs, Rumanians, Armenians, Georgians and Egyptian Copts—all belonged to the various Christian churches, of which by far the most important was the Orthodox. In addition there were the Jews who at this time were migrating in large numbers to the lands of the sultan because they found there a degree of religious tolerance unknown and unimaginable in the Christian Europe of that day. All in all, a population of approximately fifty millions compared to the five millions in contemporary England.

The sultan was the supreme ruler of these lands and peoples. Although generally regarded as a despot, his despotism in fact was rigidly limited by a specific and immutable constitution. This constitution, known as the *Sheri*, or Sacred Law of Islam, was based upon the word of God—the Koran—and upon the sayings of Mohammed—the Hadith. The *Sheri* was not merely a religious law like the canon law of Christendom. It left no scope for secular laws to regulate mundane affairs. It was theoretically adequate to govern the Islamic world and to regulate minutely the social, ethical, religious and economic life of all its members.

In actual practice the *Sheri* soon became obsolete, at least as a political constitution. It was designed to regulate the primitive society of the Arabian Peninsula rather than the world empire that Islam soon conquered. Furthermore this Sacred Law, believed to be of divine origin, was unchangeable by its own provisions. Judges and jurists attempted to provide elasticity through interpretation, but this procedure by itself was insufficient. Accordingly the sultans supplemented the Sacred Law by decrees of their own known as *kanuns*. These decrees did not constitute a secular law rivalling the *Sheri*. They were merely regulations applying to matters undefined by the *Sheri*, with the precepts of which they could not conflict. These *kanuns* allowed the sultans a certain latitude, though it was quite limited and rigidly circumscribed. No *kanun* could be effective unless it received the support of the conservative Moslem population and unless it were approved by the decisions of the established heads of law and religion, known collectively as the *ulema*. The latter, in fact, more than once forced the deposition of sultans who were judged to have violated the Sacred Law.

These restrictions left the head of the Ottoman Empire with little legislative power. But his administrative authority was virtually absolute, and the reason was that the administration and the standing army were composed almost entirely of slaves over whom the sultan had the power of life and death. The use of slaves was not uncommon in Moslem states, especially for military purposes. The Ottoman rulers from an early period maintained a standing army of slaves in addition to a feudal cavalry force composed of free-born Moslem landholders. . . . The greater part of the Ottoman armed forces consisted of a feudal territorial cavalry known as *spahis*. These were meritorious Moslem soldiers to whom the sultan granted the right to collect certain taxes from specified villages. This was the equivalent of a settled income, in return for which the incumbent was required to reside on the land and to be ready to give war service at a moment's notice. The size of the fief determined the number of extra armed horsemen that the *spahi* was required to bring to battle. . . .

This arrangement superficially resembled the feudal system of western Europe. In practice it was much more centralized and efficient when the empire was at its height. The *spahis* were required to serve as long as they were needed in contrast to the forty days per year limitation common in the West. The *spahis* also paid allegiance to only one lord, their sultan, and no subinfeudation was allowed to weaken this relationship. Furthermore the *spahis* were directly supervised by the sultan's slaves sent out from Constantinople to administer the provinces. These officials were of several ranks, the highest being the *sanjak bey* who governed a district or *sanjak,* and the *beylerbey* who had authority over all the beys of his province.

The central government did not pay these administrators regular salaries from the treasury. Instead it attached fiefs to the offices, and the proceeds of the fiefs were available for the support of the officeholders. The latter, therefore, were feudal landholders themselves, but only in a limited sense—only by virtue of their office and for the duration of their tenure. Fiefs were set aside not only for administrative offices but also for numerous military posts, for members of the imperial family, and for the sultan's private domain. Thus the *spahis,* who alone enjoyed hereditary rights, controlled less than half of the enfeoffed land. This in turn meant that Otto-man feudalism was correspondingly more centralized than that in the West. . . .

A basic difference between the Ruling and Moslem Institutions was that the former was slave-manned, whereas the latter of necessity was exclusively Moslem. The core of the Moslem Institution com-prised those true believers who were experts in their knowledge of the Koran and who served as teachers, as judges, and as jurist-the-ologians.

The teachers taught in schools which were usually attached to mosques and which were in three grades: primary schools (*mektebs*), colleges (*medressehs*) and law schools of university grade (higher *medressehs*). The graduates of the colleges were eligible to teach in the primary schools and to attend to ecclesiastical duties. Those who completed the long and arduous course in the law schools could choose one of several callings: they might become professors of law in their turn, or they might join the select and distinguished class of jurists or enter the judicial system. In the latter case they would be appointed as judges or *kazis*. . . . The law they admin-istered was the Sacred Law supplemented by the *kanuns* of the sul-tans and the customs of the regions in which they served. Con-temporary western observers were impressed by the speed and definiteness with which the *kazis* settled their cases, though they also reported that bribery and corruption were as common as in their own countries.

Those university graduates who became jurists ranked the highest in public esteem. These jurists or *muftis* were assigned as counsellors to the *kazis* of every important city and to the *sanjak beys* and *beylerbeys*. The function they fulfilled had no exact parallel in western society. Appointed for life, the *muftis* lived in retirement and could not take the initiative on any issue. Rather they served as a sort of court of appeal or reference. If a judge or a *bey* or any private citizen faced a problem involving knowledge of the Sacred Law, he would refer it to the *mufti*. The latter, after careful con-sideration, gave his professional opinion or *fetva*, which usually settled the case. The mufti of Constantinople, known as the *Sheik ul-Islam*, was the highest religious and legal authority of the empire. His position might be compared to that of the Supreme Court of the United States. He interpreted and defended the Sacred Law, the Ottoman equivalent of the American Constitution. In a sense he stood above the sultan himself. He could pass judgment, if requested, upon any action or legislation by the sultan, and if he found it a violation of the Sacred Law, the sultan then could rightfully be deposed. . . .

All these teachers, judges and jurists, known collectively as the *ulema* or learned men, had an identical training and a common philosophy of life. They were the exponents and guardians of the Sacred Law. And since this inflexible body of doctrine was essentially hostile to change and progress, the Moslem Institution became the instrument of a blighting bondage upon the empire and its peoples. Whereas the western world emancipated itself from a comparable scholasticism, the Ottoman Empire, partly because of the influence of the Moslem Institution, remained in servitude until the nineteenth century. In short, the *ulema* gave the empire a monolithic unity which at first was impressive and effective but which in the long run proved a fatal millstone.

Having considered both the Moslem and Ruling Institutions, we turn finally to the Divan, the body that brought them both together and gave unity to the organization of the empire. The early sultans presided in person over the meetings of the Divan, but Suleiman and his successors usually delegated this function to their grand vizirs. The latter were the sultans' "burdenbearers" in fact as well as in name. They supervised the entire imperial administration, both central and provincial. They controlled the army, and were expected to lead it in the field if necessary. Together with the *kaziaskers* (chief judges), they served as a supreme court of justice. And throughout the year they presided over long sessions of the Divan four days each week.

The Divan consisted of *ex officio* members who represented both Institutions. The *kaziaskers* of Europe and Asia represented the Moslem Institution. Their counterparts from the Ruling Institution were the two administrative heads, the *beylerbeys* of Europe and Asia, and the two financial heads, the *defterdars* of Europe and Asia. The latter were the treasurers of the empire, responsible for all incoming and outgoing funds. The janissaries were represented by their general or *agha,* and the naval forces by their admiral or *kapudan pasha.* Finally there was the *nishanji,* the head of the imperial chancery which made and preserved a record of every act of the government.

The Divan transacted an enormous amount of business with efficiency and dispatch. Discussion was brief and to the point, the Turks being traditionally close-tongued. All decisions were submitted to the approval of the sultan, but when this was given they were irrevocable. Since the Sacred Law was the constitution of the empire, the Divan had no legislative authority. But it was the top judicial and administrative organ of the state—the capstone of the Moslem and Ruling Institutions.

4 / THE JANISSARIES AND THE OTTOMAN ARMY

The apparent invincibility of the Ottoman Army disturbed Christian observers, who were impressed above all by the discipline and exploits of the Janissaries. Though small in numbers, they seemed to be the chief source of Turkish military strength. Among those who saw something of them at first hand was Ogier Ghiselin de Busbecq, a Flemish aristocrat who served as the Emperor Ferdinand's ambassador to Constantinople from 1555 to 1562. His Four Turkish Letters, published in Latin at Paris in 1589, gave so brilliant a picture of Turkish life and institutions that the book went rapidly through many editions and was translated into the principal languages of Europe. His comments on the Janissaries are reproduced below.

At Buda I made my first acquaintance with the Janissaries; this is the name by which the Turks call the infantry of the royal guard. The Turkish state has 12,000 of these troops when the corps is at its full strength. They are scattered through every part of the empire, either to garrison the forts against the enemy, or to protect the Christians and Jews from the violence of the mob. There is no district with any considerable amount of population, no borough or city, which has not a detachment of Janissaries to protect Christians, Jews and other helpless people from outrage and wrong.

A garrison of Janissaries is always stationed in the citadel of Buda. The dress of the men consists of a robe reaching down to

From *The Life and Letters of Ogier Ghiselin de Busbecq,* trans. Foster & Daniell, London, 1881, vol. 1, pp. 86-87.

the ankles, while to cover their heads, they employ a cowl which, by their account, was originally a cloak sleeve, part of which contains the head, while the remainder hangs down and flaps against the neck. On their forehead is placed a silver-gilt cone of considerable height, studded with stones of great value.

The Turkish monarch going to war takes with him over 20,000 camels and nearly as many baggage mules, of which a great part are loaded with rice and other kinds of grain. These mules and camels also serve to carry tents and armour, and likewise tools and munitions for the campaign. . . . The invading army carefully abstains from encroaching on its magazines at the outset; as they are well aware that when the season for campaigning draws to a close, they will have to retreat over districts wasted by the enemy, or scraped bare by countless hordes of men and droves of hungry animals, as if they had been devastated by locusts; accordingly they reserve their stores as much as possible for this emergency. Then the Sultan's magazines are opened, and a ration just sufficient to sustain life is daily weighed out to the Janissaries and other troops of the royal household. The rest of the army is badly off, unless they have provided some supplies at their own expense. . . . On such occasions they take out a few spoonfuls of flour and put them into water, adding some butter, and seasoning the mess with salt and spices; these ingredients are boiled, and a large bowl of gruel is thus obtained. Of this they eat once or twice a day, according to the quantity they have, without any bread, unless they have brought some biscuit with them. . . . Sometimes they have recourse to horseflesh; dead horses are of course plentiful in their great hosts, and such beasts as are in good condition when they die furnish a meal not to be despised by famished soldiers.

From this you will see that it is the patience, self-denial and thrift of the Turkish soldier that enable him to face the most trying circumstances and come safely out of the dangers that surround him. What a contrast to our men! Christian soldiers on a campaign refuse to put up with their ordinary food, and call for thrushes, becaficos [a small bird esteemed a dainty, as it feeds on figs and grapes], and suchlike dainty dishes! . . . It makes me shudder to think of what the result of a struggle between such different systems must be; one of us must prevail and the other be destroyed, at any rate we cannot both exist in safety. On their side is the vast wealth of their empire, unimpaired resources, experience and practice in arms, a veteran soldiery, an uninterrupted series of victories, readiness to endure hardships, union, order, discipline, thrift and watchfulness. On ours are found an empty exchequer, luxurious habits, exhausted resources, broken spirits, a raw and insubordinate soldiery, and greedy quarrels; there is no regard for discipline, license runs riot, the men indulge in drunkenness and debauchery, and worst of all, the enemy are accustomed to victory, we to defeat. Can we doubt what the result must be? The only obstacle is Persia, whose position on his rear forces the invader to take precautions. The fear of Persia gives us a respite, but it is only for a time.

5 / RELIGIOUS MINORITIES IN THE OTTOMAN EMPIRE

True to the law of Islam, the Turks accorded full toleration to Christians and Jews, who were organized in millets, *religious communities, and allowed to govern themselves under their own chiefs and customs. They had the status of* dhimmis, *"protected persons," but were socially segregated from Muslims and rarely learned to speak the Turkish language. The Turks, it may be said, identified themselves more closely with Islam than even the Arabs: A non-Muslim Turk was, and still is, virtually a contradiction in terms. The following account of the position of religious minorities in the Ottoman Empire is from a work by an English scholar.*

From the earliest days of the extension of their kingdom in Asia Minor, the Ottomans exercised authority over Christian subjects, but it was not until the ancient capital of the Eastern empire fell into their hands in 1453 that the relations between the Muslim Government and the Christian Church were definitely established on a fixed basis. One of the first steps taken by Muhammad II after the capture of Constantinople and the re-establishment of order in that city was to secure the allegiance of the Christians by proclaiming himself the protector of the Greek Church. Persecution of the Christians was strictly forbidden; a decree was granted to the newly elected patriarch which secured to him and his successors, and the bishops under him, the enjoyment of the old privileges, revenues

From *The Preaching of Islam* by T. W. Arnold, Luzac and Co., London, 1896, pp. 145-56.

and exemptions enjoyed under the former rule. Gennadios, the first patriarch after the Turkish conquest, received from the hands of the Sultan himself the pastoral staff, which was the sign of his office, together with a purse of a thousand golden ducats and a horse with gorgeous trappings, on which he was privileged to ride with his train through the city. But not only was the head of the Church treated with all the respect he had been accustomed to receive from the Christian emperors, but further he was invested with extensive civil power. The patriarch's court sat to decide all cases between Greek and Greek; it could impose fines, imprison offenders in a prison provided for its own special use, and in some cases even condemn to capital punishment: while the ministers and officials of the government were directed to enforce its judgments. The complete control of spiritual and ecclesiastical matters (in which the Turkish government, unlike the civil power of the Byzantine empire, never interfered), was left entirely in his hands and those of the grand Synod which he could summon whenever he pleased; and hereby he could decide all matters of faith and dogma without fear of interference on the part of the state. As a recognised officer of the imperial government, he could do much for the alleviation of the oppressed, by bringing the acts of unjust governors to the notice of the Sultan. The Greek bishops in the provinces in their turn were treated with great consideration and were entrusted with so much jurisdiction in civil affairs, that up to modern times they have acted in their dioceses almost as if they were Ottoman prefects over the orthodox population, and we find that the higher clergy were generally more active as Turkish agents than as Greek priests, and they always taught their people that the Sultan possessed a divine sanction, as the protector of the Orthodox Church. A charter was subsequently published, securing to the orthodox the use of such churches as had not been confiscated to form mosques, and authorising them to celebrate their religious rites publicly according to their national usages.

Consequently, though the Greeks were numerically superior to the Turks in all the European provinces of the empire, the religious toleration thus granted them, and the protection of life and property they enjoyed, soon reconciled them to the change of masters and led them to prefer the domination of the Sultan to that of any Christian power. Indeed, in many parts of the country, the Ottoman conquerors were welcomed by the Greeks as their deliverers from the rapacious and tyrannous rule of the Franks and Venetians. . . . For at least a century after the fall of Constantinople a series of able rulers secured, by a firm and vigorous administration, peace and order throughout their dominions, and an admirable civil and judicial organisation, if it did not provide an absolutely impartial justice for Muslims and Christians alike, yet caused the Greeks to be far better off than they had been before. . . . The Turkish dominions were certainly better governed and more prosperous than most parts of Christian Europe, and the mass of the Christian population engaged in the cultivation of the soil enjoyed a larger measure of private liberty and of the fruits of their labour, under the government of the Sultan than their contemporaries did under that of many Christian monarchs. . . .

If we except the tribute of the children, to which the conquered Greeks seem to have submitted with so little show of resistance, the treatment of their Christian subjects by the Ottoman emperors—at least for two centuries after their conquest of Greece—exhibits a toleration such as was at that time quite unknown in the rest of Europe. The Calvinists of Hungary and Transylvania, and the Unitarians of the latter country, long preferred to submit to the Turks rather than fall into the hands of the fanatical house of Hapsburg; and the Protestants of Silesia looked with longing eyes towards Turkey, and would gladly have purchased religious freedom at the price of submission to the Muslim rule. It was to Turkey that the persecuted Spanish Jews fled for refuge in enormous numbers at the end of the fifteenth century, and the Cossacks who belonged to the sect of the Old Believers and were persecuted by the Russian State Church, found in the dominions of the Sultan the toleration which their Christian brethren denied them.

6 / MUHAMMAD THE CONQUEROR

The greatest of the Ottoman sultans was Muhammad II (1451-81), who earned his title "the Conqueror" by capturing Constantinople in 1453. For years he was the terror of Europe; when he died in 1481, his troops had gained a footing in Italy and taken Otranto, and to many it seemed that Old Rome might go the way of New

Rome. Hard and cruel, he was nonetheless a man of culture, and his life and career present some curious links with the Italian Renaissance. He knew Greek, a Greek scholar (Critoboulos) wrote his biography, and a Venetian artist (Gentile Bellini) painted his portrait. Richard Knolles, a Kentish schoolmaster who wrote a history of the Turks in the reign of Elizabeth I, here gives a striking and balanced picture of this deadly enemy of Christendom.

The death of this mighty man (who living troubled a great part of the world) was not much more lamented by those that were nearest unto him (who, ever living in fear of his cruelty, hated him deadly) than [the death] of his enemies, who ever in doubt of his greatness, were glad to hear of his end. He was of stature but low, and nothing answerable to the height of his mind, square set, and strongly limbed; not inferior in strength (when he was young) unto any in his father's court; his complexion was Tartar-like, sallow and melancholy, as were most of his ancestors the Othoman kings; his look and countenance stern, with his eyes piercing, hollow and little sunk as it were in his head, and his nose so high and crooked that it almost touched his upper lip. To be brief, his countenance was altogether such, as if nature had with most cunning hand therein depainted [depicted] and most curiously set forth to view the inward disposition and qualities of his mind: which were on both parts notable. He was of a very sharp and apprehensive wit, learned as amongst that nation, especially in astronomy, and could speak the Greek, Latin, Arabic, Chaldee [Syriac?], and Persian tongues. He delighted much in reading of histories, and the lives of worthy men, especially the lives of Alexander the Great and Julius Caesar, whom he proposed to himself as examples to follow. He was of an exceeding courage, and thereto very fortunate: a severe punisher of injustice, in them especially to whom he had committed the administration of justice. Men that excelled in any quality, he greatly favored and honorably entertained, as he did Gentile Bellini, a painter of Venice, whom he purposely caused to come from thence to Constantinople, to draw the lively counterfeit of himself, for which he most bountifully rewarded him. He so severely punished theft, as that in his time all the ways were safe, and a thief scarcely to be

From *A Generall Historie of the Turkes* by Richard Knolles. London, 1603, p. 433. (Spelling modernized.)

heard of. But these good parts were in him obscured with most horrible and notorious vices: for why, he was altogther irreligious, and of all others most perfidious, ambitious above measure, and in nothing more delighted than in blood: insomuch that it is probably gathered, that he was in his time [responsible for] the death of 800,000 men: craft, covetousness and dissimulation were in him accounted for tolerable faults, in comparison of his greater vices. In his love was no assurance, and his least displeasure was death: so that he lived feared of all men, and died lamented of none.

7 / THE TURKISH SIEGE OF VIENNA, 1529

Sultan Sulaiman, on ascending the throne in 1520, resumed the Muslim war on Christendom almost at the point at which it had been left off on the death of Muhammad II in 1481. He drove the Knights of St. John from the island of Rhodes in 1522, led a great expedition across the Danube into Hungary, and overthrew the king and nobility of that kingdom on the field of Mohacs in 1526. The fall of Hungary opened the road to Austria and the German lands, already thrown into confusion by the religious schism of the Reformation; and in 1529 the Sultan advanced at the head of a large army toward the imperial capital of Vienna. The defense of the city was in the hands of the Archduke Ferdinand, brother of the Emperor Charles V, who now claimed the crown of Hungary. To this move Sulaiman responded by supporting the claim of John Zapolya, whom he planned to make a puppet king under Turkish suzerainty. Had Vienna fallen, all Central Europe might have passed under Ottoman control. As it was, the Turks were repulsed from its walls, and their failure marked the limit of their advance into Europe. Ottoman expansion on land was halted, and the Turkish system of government geared to the needs of a militant frontier society, began to run down. An American historian here tells the story of the failure of the first Ottoman siege of Vienna.

On May 10, 1529, [Sulaiman] left Constantinople at the head of a much larger army than that of 1526. The Christian chroniclers talk vaguely of 250,000 to 300,000, though it is doubtful if there were more than 75,000 fighting men, and it seems clear that four-fifths of them were cavalry. Ibrahim was again *seraskier* (commander-

From *Suleiman the Magnificent* by R. B. Merriman, pp. 104-108. Copyright 1944 by Harvard University Press. Reprinted with permission of the publisher.

in-chief), and the artillery is given as before at 300 guns. The rains, which in the preceding campaign had been a nuisance, were this year so continuous and torrential that they seriously affected the outcome of the campaign. Suleiman did not reach Vienna till a month later than he expected, and that month may well have made just the difference between failure and success. The Sultan's comments in his diary on the bad weather are constant and bitter. At Mohacs on August 18 he had been joined by Zapolya, whose prospects had speedily revived when it became known that he had won the favour of Suleiman. He brought with him 6000 men. The Sultan received him with great pomp, and presented him with four robes of honour and three horses caparisoned with gold. But Suleiman in his diary takes great pains to point out that he regarded him merely as a vassal. He explains that the gifts were only bestowed in recognition of the voivode's homage; and he emphasizes the fact that Zapolya twice kissed his hand. At Buda a feeble resistance was offered by a few hundred Austrian mercenaries, but they soon surrendered after a promise of good treatment, which was shamefully violated by the Janissaries. Zapolya was permitted to make a royal entrance there on September 14; but he was obviously dominated and controlled by the Turkish soldiers and officials who escorted him, and Ludovico Gritti was left behind as the Sultan's representative. Gran, Dotis, Komorn and Raab either surrendered or were evacuated. Pressburg, which alone seemed likely to offer serious resistance, was by-passed. On September 18 the *akinji* (irregular cavalry) swarmed across the Austrian frontier, and swept like a hurricane through the open country. On the 27th the Sultan himself arrived before Vienna. Two days later the investment was complete.

Ferdinand had had plenty of time to prepare, but it proved difficult to find means. His ancestral lands granted grudging subsidies, but he could do nothing without help from outside. His brother Charles was anxious to aid him, but was unable to gain peace with Francis I till August 5, too late to set free the imperial troops in Italy. Ferdinand's best hope was the princes of the Empire, then assembled at the Diet of Spires, and thither he at once repaired, to assure them that if Austria were conquered, it would be Germany's turn next. But the Diet hesitated. The problem that occupied its chief attention at the time was that of the Lutherans.

The Saxon Reformer had recently come out with a pamphlet, "On the War against the Turks," in which he sought to correct any misconstruction of his earlier words on the subject by exhorting all princes to stand by the Emperor for the defense of Christendom. The tract was somewhat half-hearted: one could not help feeling that Luther still regarded Rome as a more serious menace than the Ottoman; nevertheless it ultimately served to help persuade Catholics and Protestants to unite in voting a *Reichshilfe* or quota for the defence of the Empire. The collection of the troops took many weeks. Had not the Sultan been delayed by the rains, they could scarcely have arrived on time; but three days before Suleiman reached Vienna, sufficient reinforcements had appeared on the scene to raise the number of the garrison from about 12,000 to nearly 20,000 men. The greater part of them, moreover, were professional soldiers, veterans who loved war. Count Nicholas von Salm, who had already fought the Turks and had recently distinguished himself at the battle of Pavia, was in chief command. Ferdinand was at Prague during the crucial weeks of the campaign.

The siege of Vienna appeals strongly to the imagination. Never since the battle of Tours, almost precisely eight centuries before, had Christian Europe been so direfully threatened by Mohammedan Asia and Africa. Had the verdict on either occasion been reversed, the whole history of the world might have been changed. And the cause of the Moslem defeat in both cases was fundamentally the same; the invaders had outrun their communications. This is well demonstrated in the case of Vienna by the fact that the long distances and heavy rains had forced the Turks to leave behind them the bulk of their heavy artillery, which had been such a decisive factor in the siege of Rhodes. The lighter cannon, which was almost all they succeeded in bringing with them, could make little impression on the city walls. Only by mining operations could they hope to open a breach for a general assault.

The Vienna of 1529 was not much more than what is to-day contained within the *Ring* or *Ringstrasse*. On the north-east side it was protected by what is now called the Donau canal, or southern arm of the Danube, and on the south-east by its little tributary the Wiener-Bach. The city was surrounded by a medieval wall, considerably strengthened during the weeks before the Turks arrived, and the defenders possessed an admirable watchtower in the tall spire of St. Stephen, whence all the movements of the besiegers could be observed; Count von Salm spent much of his time there. The Turks soon saw that the most promising place to attack was the "Karinthner Thor" or Carinthian Gate, on the south side of the city, to the west of the Wiener-Bach, and there they concentrated the mass of their forces. The Sultan's headquarters were his splendid red tent, pitched on a hill, three or four miles away. Mining and counter-mining operations were vigorously pushed during the early days of October. Several times the besiegers were encouraged to launch assaults, which were invariably repulsed. On the other hand, the constant sorties of the garrison were generally unsuccessful. October 12 was the critical day of the siege. On that morning the walls had been breached by mines, and the Turks had delivered the most furious of their attacks. Only with great difficulty had it been beaten off, and the garrison was deeply discouraged; that very afternoon it dispatched the most pressing of its messages to hasten the arrival of relief. But the Turks were in even worse case. At the Divan [council] which they held that same day the preponderance of opinion was in favour of withdrawal. The season was ominously late; supplies were getting short; the Janissaries were murmuring; powerful Christian reinforcements were known to be at hand. Ibrahim besought his master to go home. One more last attack was launched on October 14, but despite the unprecedented rewards that had been offered in case it should be successful, it was delivered in such half-hearted fashion that it was foredoomed to failure from the first. That night the Turks massacred some 2000 of the prisoners that they had taken from the Austrian countryside; they burnt their own encampment; on the 15th they began to retire. Their retreat was cruelly harassed by enemy cavalry, and truly horrible weather pursued them all the way to Constantinople. It was cold comfort that Zapolya came out from Buda as the Sultan passed by to compli-ment his master on his "successful campaign." All that the Sultan had succeeded in doing was to expel Ferdinand from his Hungarian dominions; and we need not take too seriously the statement in his diary that since he had learnt the archduke was not in Vienna, he had lost all interest in capturing the place! The fundamental fact remained that Suleiman had been beaten back before the walls of the Austrian capital by a force a third the size of his own, or perhaps less.

II / SAFAVID PERSIA

INTRODUCTION

The revolution in Persia at the turn of the fifteenth and sixteenth centuries altered the history of Islam and may almost be said to have been the salvation of Europe. It distracted the attention of the Ottoman Turks from Christendom and opened a schism in the Muslim world which has not yet been closed.

Persia is a land of ancient culture, whose historical memories go back to Cyrus the Great in the sixth century B.C. For four hundred years (A.D. 226-651) she was governed by a native dynasty, the Sassanids, whose achievements have been kept alive in the national tradition. The Arab conquest in the seventh century not only overthrew this dynasty, but temporarily destroyed Persia as a national state. After a time, the Persian genius reasserted itself, and Persia took captive her conquerors, as the Greeks had the Romans. While accepting Islam, the Persians interpreted it in their own fashion and almost took it out of Arab hands. Most of the leading Muslim theologians were Persian, as were most of the poets, historians, geographers, and scientists of Islam's golden age, and the remarkable movement of Sufi mysticism was very largely a Persian creation. For two or three centuries after the Arab conquest, Persian scholars and men of letters wrote in Arabic, but in the tenth century a new form of written Persian emerged and was stabilized as a literary language by the great Firdawsi, whose *Shahnamah,* or *Book of Kings,* is one of the world's finest epic poems. At the same time, a Persian family, the Buyids, restored native political control over the country and forced the Arab caliphs of Baghdad into dependence on them.

31

Persian steadily superseded Arabic in the schools and public services, and Persia's restoration as an independent national state seemed imminent. This did not happen, however, because of the coming of the Turks.

Relations between Persians and Turks have always been complex and usually unfriendly. The Persians, a sophisticated, literate people, regarded the Turks, who were by origin nomads from the steppes of Central Asia, as coarse, ignorant barbarians, and the two races rarely mingled. Various Turkish tribes, beginning with the Seljuks, entered Persia from the eleventh century onward and settled with their flocks and herds in the steppelike portions of the country most suitable for pasture. It would not be quite true to say that the Persians lived in cities and the Turks in the countryside, but the latter, a race of shepherds and warriors, were never really urbanized. The two peoples had at least this in common: They were both Muslim, and the Turks tended to accept the Persian version of Islam and, in particular, the doctrines and attitudes of the Shi'a.

Shi'a is an Arabic word meaning "party," and was originally applied to those Muslims who thought that Muhammad's cousin and son-in-law Ali should, on the Prophet's death, have succeeded him as the first caliph and that the men who did succeed him, namely, Abu Bakr, Omar, and Othman, were usurpers. Ali did become caliph after Othman's death, but his reign was short, and his family were thrust aside by successful rivals, first the Omayyads and then the Abbasids. His supporters argued that Ali's line had a divine right to the caliphate, but the party split on the question of which particular line of descent should be followed. Some espoused the claim of those descended from Isma'il, of the seventh generation from Ali, and so were known as "Seveners" or "Isma'ilians"; others fixed on the twelfth and hence were styled "Twelvers."

It is noteworthy that the Shi'a held a view of political power quite different from that of the Sunnites, or orthodox Muslims. To the latter, a Muslim prince, king, or even caliph was only a civil magistrate charged with the defense of Islam and its Law; to the Shi'a, the Muslim community must be governed by an Imam, or holy leader, of the house of Ali, who is the direct representative of God on earth and the infallible interpreter of the Divine Law.

Before 1500 the politico-religious quarrel between the Shi'ites and the Sunnites was not very acute in Persia. Most of the townsfolk were probably Sunnite, though certain districts, especially in north Persia, were traditionally Shi'ite in sympathy. Twelver Shi'ism had much support among the nomadic or seminomadic Turkoman tribes, including those who grazed their flocks in Azerbaijan, a land of pasture that had been Turkish-speaking for several generations; it was propagated among them by religious leaders, holy men known as *Shaikhs sayyids*—that is, those who claimed descent from the Prophet through Fatima—, who were treated with great respect and veneration by the simple, primitive herdsmen. One of these shaikhs, Safi al-Din, a name meaning "Purity of the Faith," who founded a kind of religious order in Gilan, a hill province south of the Caspian Sea, gave his name to the Safavid dynasty. He died in 1334, and his heirs conducted a vigorous Shi'ite propaganda, their adherents acquiring the nickname of *Kizil-bash,* or "Red Caps," from the distinctively colored headgear they adopted as a badge of membership. In the troubles which followed the death of Usun Hasan in 1478, the Safavids seized the chance to grasp at political power. They enlisted the aid of Turkoman troops and launched an armed rising in the name of Safi's descendant Isma'il, a precocious boy of thirteen or fourteen. In 1500 the Red Caps entered Tabriz, the capital of Azerbaijan, where Isma'il was proclaimed Shah and Imam, and a new era began in the history of Islam.

8 / THE RISE OF THE SAFAVIDS

The advent of the young Shah Isma'il is described and commented on by Edward G. Browne, the distinguished British orientalist and author of the classic Literary History of Persia, *from which the following extract is taken.*

The rapid rise to power of Isma'il is one of the most remarkable events in Persian history, especially in view of his forlorn and threatened childhood. His father, Shaikh Haydar, was killed in A.D. 1490, when he was only about three years of age, and he and his two brothers, of whom the elder, Sultan Ali, also fell in battle about A.D. 1495, were in constant danger from the Turkmen rulers of the

From *A Literary History of Persia,* by Edward G. Browne, vol. 4, pp. 21-22. Copyright 1924 by the Cambridge University Press, England. Reprinted with permission of the Hon. Sir Patrick Browne and Mr. Michael Browne.

"White Sheep" dynasty, and had many hair-breadth escapes in which they owed their lives to the devoted loyalty of their faithful Sufis. Only seven of these accompanied Isma'il when at the age of thirteen he set out from Lahijan to Ardabil to win a kingdom or perish in the attempt, but at every stage he received reinforcements, so that at Tarum his army numbered 1500 men, and by the time he reached Arzinjan on his way to attack Farrukh-Yasan, king of Shirwan, it had increased to 7000. Within a year he had taken Tabriz, been crowned king of Persia, and despite the attempt of his counsellors to dissuade him, imposed the Shi'a doctrine on his subjects. He was warned that two-thirds of the people of Tabriz were Sunnis, and that the introduction into the prayers and professions of Faith of the distinctly Shi'a clauses, and more especially the cursing of the first three Caliphs, Abu Bakr, Umar [Omar] and Uthman [Othman], might lead to trouble. "God and the Immaculate Imams are with me," he replied, "and I fear no one. By God's help, if the people utter one word of protest, I will draw the sword and leave not one of them alive!" He was as good as his word, and when the above-mentioned anathema was uttered, all men were commanded, on the pain of death, to exclaim, "May it (i.e., the curse) be more, not less."

9 / THE EARLIEST EUROPEAN ACCOUNTS
OF SHAH ISMA'IL

The Safavid revolution aroused great interest in Europe, especially among the Venetians and Portuguese. It was soon realised that this was no mere change of dynasty but the coming of a strange new theocracy under a king who claimed almost divine powers. The success of Isma'il and his Red Caps excited the Shi'ite "orders" in Iraq and Asia Minor and seriously alarmed the Ottoman government, which began to fear the possible loss of its Asiatic dominions. The Venetians, who had suffered a series of naval defeats at Ottoman hands, were eager to make contact with the new Persian regime in order to encourage it to attack the Turks. Hence, a series of Venetian missions visited Persia soon after 1500, and their reports constitute the earliest European accounts of Shah Isma'il, "the Sophy" as they called him, and of the nature of his government. The great Portuguese Viceroy Affonso de Albuquerque, faced with an Egyptian Mamluk naval challenge in the Indian Ocean, also

sought an alliance with the Safavids, and one of his officials, Duarte
Barbosa (who afterwards entered the service of Spain and was killed
with Magellan in the Philippines in 1521), compiled a general sur-
vey of the foundation of Portuguese colonial power in Asia and
included in it a section on Shah Isma'il. Thee short Venetian eye-
witness reports are here given, followed by the passage on Isma'il
from The Book of Duarte Barbosa.

Isma'il was thirteen years old, of noble presence and a truly royal
bearing, as in his eyes and brows there was something I know not
what, so great and commanding, which plainly showed that he
would yet some day become a great ruler. Nor did the virtues of
his mind disaccord with the beauty of his person, as he had an
elevated genius and such a lofty idea of things as seemed incredible
at such a tender age. The good priest who professed to be an as-
trologer and to know the course of events from the aspect of the
heavens, cast his horoscope and foresaw that he would become lord
of all Asia. . . . He had vigour of mind, quickness of perception,
and a personal valour which he had never yet seen equalled among
his contemporaries . . . [CATERINO ZENO]

This Sophi is fair, handsome and very pleasing; not very tall, but
of a light and well-framed figure; rather stout than slight, with
broad shoulders. His hair is reddish; he only wears moustachios,
and uses his left hand instead of his right. He is as brave as a game-
cock, and stronger than any of his lords; in the archery contests,
out of ten apples that are knocked down, he knocks down seven;
while he is at his sport they play on various instruments and sing
his praises. [GIOVAN ANGIOLELLO]

Before I left Tabriz, Ismail returned with his army, for whose
coming there were great preparations made, and all the shops decorated for the festival and triumphs. He came every day to the
maidan [large open ground where military exercises are held] to
divert himself with archery with his lords who received many gifts
from him. And there was dancing, music and songs in honour of
the great Sultan Ismail when he was present in the *maidan*. This

From *Italian Travels to Tana and Persia* (ed.) C. Grey. The Hakluyt Society,
London, 1873, pp. 46-48, 111, 206. Reprinted with permission of the Hakluyt Society.

Sophy is loved and reverenced by his people as a god, and especially by his soldiers, many of whom enter the battle without armour, expecting their master Ismail to watch over them in the fight. There are also others to go into battle without armour, being willing to die for their monarch, rushing on with naked breasts, crying "Schiac, schiac [Shaikh, shaikh]." The name of God is forgotten throughout Persia, and only that of Ismail remembered; if anyone fall when riding or dismounted, he appeals to no other god but Schiac, using the name in two ways; first as god Schiac; secondly, as prophet; as the Mussulmans say, "Laylla, laylla Mahamet resuralla" ["There is no god but God, and Muhammad is his apostle"], the Persians say, "Laylla, laylla Ismael vellialla" ["There is no god but God, and Isma'il is his *wali* (friend)"]; besides this, everyone, and particularly his soldiers, consider him immortal, but I have heard that Ismail is not pleased with being called a god or a prophet. [AN ANONYMOUS MERCHANT]

From here on all are in subjection to the Xeque [Shaikh] Ismael. He is a young Moor who has of late attained this high position, and has brought under his rule a great part of Arabia and Persia, and many kingdoms and seignories of the Moors, not being a king nor the son of a king but only the son of a Xeque of the lineage of Ali. He being yet a child went to live with an Armenian friar who brought him up. Being then of the age of twelve years, he fled away, lest he should slay him as a Moor, and went to dwell in a certain city, where he lodged with a great lord, with whom he grew in favour, insomuch that he set him on horseback and gave him a good post. Thenceforward he began to take to himself other Moorish youths, and gathered together many people. Little by little he began to take villages, and to make gifts of the goods and the wealth which he found therein to those who followed him in such ventures, keeping nothing for himself. Seeing then that his affairs had made such a good beginning, he determined to have a badge of his own, and thereto he had made red caps of cloth dyed in grain, and delivered them to such persons as would be of his sect. And so it was that he gathered to himself a great number of followers, and then he began to take great towns and to wage many wars, yet notwithstanding this, he would not call himself king nor stay in any one kingdom. What things soever he takes in war he deals out to those who help him to win, and if he finds any persons who make no use of their wealth and do no service therewith to any, then he takes it from them and distributes it equally to the worthy men of his army whom he knows to be in want, and to the real owner of the property he gives as much as to each one of them. Hence some Moors call him "The Leveller," but his true name is Xeque Ismael, and this is his wont: he sends his ambassadors to all the Moorish kings and demands that they shall wear the red caps as his badge, and if they will not wear these badges they are to challenge them, and give them to know that he will pursue after them, and take their lands from them, and compel them to believe in him. In this manner he sent an embassy to the great Soldan [the Mamluk sultan of Egypt] and to the Grand Turk [the Ottoman sultan], who after taking counsel together, sent an evil answer by his ambassadors, determining to defend themselves against him and to render aid each to the other. Xeque Ismael then seeing their replies, at once made ready to go against the Turk with a great army of foot and horse, and so came to seek him, who on his part sallied forth to meet him, in nowise ill-arrayed. Thus between the two there was a great battle, in which the Turk was conqueror by reason of the mighty artillery which he brought with him, in which the Xeque was altogether lacking, for he and his people fight only with the strength of their arms. Here the Turks slew many of his people, and he took to flight. The Turk followed in pursuit, still slaying many, until he arrived in the land of Persia, whence he turned back to Turkey. This was the first time that Xeque Ismael had been overcome, by which he was greatly grieved, and determined to meet the Turk another time, but provided with artillery and in much greater strength than before.

This Xeque Ismael is lord over Babylonia, Armenia, the whole of Persia, a great part of Arabia, part of India, over against Cambaya [Gujarat], and his determination is to have the house of Mecca [i.e., the Ka'ba, or temple of Mecca, "the house of God"] in his hands. He sent an embassy to the Captain-in-Chief [Albuquerque] of the King our Lord [Emanuel of Portugal] with many presents, offering him alliance and peace, who received it very graciously, and sent in return another embassy and present.

III / THE SCHISM IN THE MUSLIM WORLD

INTRODUCTION

The great split which occurred in the Islamic community on the coming of the Safavids was almost as serious and far-reaching in its consequences as the Protestant Reformation, which began a few years later, was to Christendom. Isma'il resolved to turn Persia into a Shi'ite state: Ali and his house received a semidivine veneration, and the three "usurping" caliphs (Abu Bakr, Omar, and Othman) were regularly cursed from the mosque pulpits. The Turcoman tribes formed the military basis of his power; contact was made with their fellow Turcomans in the Ottoman Empire, and the Shi'ite "orders" in Asia Minor watched events in Persia with sympathetic interest. Isma'il no doubt hoped to spread his particular version of Islam throughout the Muslim world, as the Fatimids had tried to do six hundred years before, and Asia Minor seemed to offer the most promising immediate field of operations. This presented a grave challenge to the Ottomans, who were driven to adopt a strong anti-Shi'ite and anti-Safavid policy in order to save their Asiatic territories from absorption by the "heretics." The aged, pacific, and ineffective Sultan Bayezid II was shouldered out of the way by his masterful son, Selim the Grim (1512-20), who made himself the champion and spokesman of orthodox, Sunnite Islam, launched a violent persecution of Shi'ites in his realm (forty thousand reportedly having perished), and prepared a formidable military expedition against the Safavid kingdom. Before marching, he issued an arrogant and offensive manifesto, calling on Isma'il to repent of his heresies and cede certain territories which the Sultan alleged were rightfully his.

10 / SULTAN SELIM'S LETTER TO SHAH ISMA'IL, 1514

This formidable state document is preserved in a collection of Otto-man government papers made in 1574 by Feridun Bey, a chancery official.

The Supreme Being who is at once the sovereign arbiter of the destinies of men and the source of all light and knowledge, declares in the holy book [the Koran] that the true faith is that of the Muslims, and that whoever professes another religion, far from being hearkened to and saved, will on the contrary be cast out among the rejected on the great day of the Last Judgment; He says further, this God of truth, that His designs and decrees are unalterable, that all human acts are perforce reported to Him, and that he who abandons the good way will be condemned to hellfire and eternal torments. Place yourself, O Prince, among the true believers, those who walk in the path of salvation, and who turn aside with care from vice and infidelity. May the purest and holiest blessings be upon Muhammad, the master of the two worlds, the prince of prophets, as well as upon his descendants and all who follow his Law!

I, sovereign chief of the Ottomans, master of the heroes of the age, who unites the force and power of Feridun [a legendary king of ancient Persia], the majesty and glory of Alexander the Great, the justice and clemency of Khusraw [the famous King of Persia, in whose reign Muhammad was born]; I, the exterminator of idolators, destroyer of the enemies of the true faith, the terror of the tyrants and pharaohs of the age; I, before whom proud and unjust kings have humbled themselves, and whose hand breaks the strongest sceptres; I, the great Sultan-Khan, son of Sultan Bayezid-Khan, son of Sultan Muhammad-Khan, son of Sultan Murad-Khan, I address myself graciously to you, Amir Isma'il, chief of the troops of Persia, comparable in tyranny to Sohak and Afrasiab [legendary kings of Central Asia], and predestined to perish like the last Darius,

Translated by the editor from J. von Hammer, *Histoire de l'Empire Othman.* Paris, 1836, vol. 4, pp. 177-82.

in order to make known to you that the works emanating from the Almighty are not the fragile products of caprice or folly, but make up an infinity of mysteries impenetrable to the human mind. The Lord Himself says in his holy book: "We have not created the heavens and the earth in order to play a game" [Koran, 21:16]. Man, who is the noblest of the creatures and the summary of the marvels of God, is in consequence on earth the living image of the Creator. It is He who has set up Caliphs on earth, because, joining faculties of soul with perfection of body, man is the only being who can comprehend the attributes of the divinity and adore its sublime beauties; but he possesses this rare intelligence, he attains this divine knowledge only in our religion and by observing the precepts of the prince of prophets, the Caliph of Caliphs, the right arm of the God of Mercy; it is then only by practising the true religion that man will prosper in this world and merit eternal life in the other. As to you, Amir Isma'il, such a recompense will not be your lot; because you have denied the sanctity of the divine laws; because you have deserted the path of salvation and the sacred commandments; because you have impaired the purity of the dogmas of Islam; because you have dishonoured, soiled and destroyed the altars of the Lord, usurped the sceptre of the East by unlawful and tyrannical means; because coming forth from the dust, you have raised yourself by odious devices to a place shining with splendour and magnificence; because you have opened to Muslims the gates of tyranny and oppression; because you have joined iniquity, perjury and blasphemy to your sectarian impiety; because under the cloak of the hypocrite, you have sowed everywhere trouble and sedition; because you have raised the standard of irreligion and heresy; because yielding to the impulse of your evil passions, and giving yourself up without rein to the most infamous disorders, you have dared to throw off the control of Muslim laws and to permit lust and rape, the massacre of the most virtuous and respectable men, the destruction of pulpits and temples, the profanation of tombs, the ill-treatment of the *ulama,* the doctors and amirs descended from the Prophet, the repudiation of the Koran, the cursing of the legitimate Caliphs. Now as the first duty of a Muslim and above all of a pious prince is to obey the commandment, "O, you faithful who believe, be the executors of the decrees of God!" the *ulama* and our doctors have pronounced sentence of death against you, perjurer and blasphemer, and have imposed on every Muslim the sacred obligation to arm in defence of religion and destroy heresy and impiety in your person and that of all your partisans.

Animated by the spirit of this *fetwa,* conforming to the Koran the code of divine laws, and wishing on one side to strengthen Islam, on the other to liberate the lands and peoples who writhe under your yoke, we have resolved to lay aside our imperial robes in order to put on the shield and coat of mail, to raise our ever victorious banner, to assemble our invincible armies, to take up the gauntlet of the avenger, to march with our soldiers, whose sword strikes mortal blows, and whose point will pierce the enemy even to the constellation of Sagittarius. In pursuit of this noble resolution, we have entered upon the campaign, and guided by the hand of the Almighty, we hope soon to strike down your tyrannous arm, blow away the clouds of glory and grandeur which trouble your head and cause you fatal blindness, release from your despotism your trembling subjects, smother you in the end in the very mass of flames which your infernal *jinn* raises everywhere along your passage, accomplishing in this way on you the maxim which says: "He who sows discord can only reap evils and afflictions." However, anxious to conform to the spirit of the law of the Prophet, we come, before commencing war, to set out before you the words of the Koran, in place of the sword, and to exhort you to embrace the true faith; this is why we address this letter to you.

We all have a different nature, and the human race resembles mines of gold and silver. Among some, vice is deeply rooted; these are incorrigible, and one could no more draw them to virtue than one could whiten a Negro's skin; among others, vice has not become second nature; they retract their errors when they wish, by a serious return, to mortify their senses and repress their passions. The most efficacious means of remedying evil is to search the conscience deeply, to open one's eyes to faults, and to ask pardon of the God of Mercy with true sorrow and repentance. We urge you to look into yourself, to renounce your errors, and to march towards the good with a firm and courageous step; we ask further that you give up possession of the territory violently seized from our State and to which you have only illegitimate pretentions, that you deliver it back into the hands of our lieutenants and officers; and if you value your safety and repose, this should be done without delay.

But if, to your misfortune, you persist in your past conduct; if, puffed up with the idea of your power and your foolish bravado, you wish to pursue the course of your iniquities, you will see in a few days your plains covered with our tents and inundated with our battalions. Then prodigies of valour will be done, and we shall see the decrees of the Almighty, Who is the God of Armies, and sovereign judge of the actions of men, accomplished. For the rest, victory to him who follows the path of salvation!

11 / THE BATTLE OF CHALDIRAN, 1514

The Ottoman invasion of Persia resulted in the defeat of Shah Isma'il in August 1514 at Chaldiran in northern Azerbaijan, mainly due to the superiority of the Turks in numbers and artillery. But Selim, though he captured Tabriz, was unable to follow up his victory, partly because of uncertainty concerning the attitude of the Mamluks in Egypt and Syria, partly because of unrest among the Janissaries, many of whom were under the influence of the Shi'ite dervish orders. He therefore withdrew his forces rather than risk a possible mutiny. Nonetheless, the battle proved decisive. It stopped a Safavid advance westward and left Asia Minor firmly in Ottoman possession; it sealed the fate of the Mamluks, whom Selim now came to regard as a threat to Ottoman security and resolved to destroy, and it left Twelver Shi'ism more or less confined to Persia, as it is today. It also helped to purge the Safavid regime of its universalist elements, and during the long reign of Isma'il's successor, Tahmasp I (1524-76), Persia grew imperceptibly into something like a national state, which it was not at the outset, though Turkish long remained the language of the court.

A contemporary report of the battle is furnished by the Venetian envoy Angiolello, who notes that Isma'il was handicapped by trouble with the Kurds in Iraq and the Uzbeks on his eastern frontier.

While the Sophi was in Tauris [Tabriz], some of his tributary chiefs in the territory bordering on the Turks, seeing that the army was in Corassan [Khurasan], came to an understanding with the Ottoman, and invited him to attack Persia; but for which invita-

From *Italian Travels in Persia*, ed. by C. Grey. The Hakluyt Society. London, 1873, pp. 118-20. Reprinted with permission of the Hakluyt Society.

tion the Turk would never have mustered courage to do so. Being summoned by such great chiefs and principally by the Curds [Kurds], who were enemies of the Sophi monarch, and thinking that the Sophi would be in difficulties, he determined in 1514 to form an army and invade Persia, apprehensive that if the Sophi were victorious against the Tartars [i.e., the Uzbeks of Central Asia], he would make an alliance with the Soldan [i.e., the Mamluk sultan of Egypt] for his destruction. Hence he set out from Constantinople and made his way with a great number of men to Amasia. . . . He reached Sivas, making great booty, and sending many people to Amasia and Constantinople, principally artisans and skilled workmen, and also men of rank. The Sophi, who was in Tauris, hearing this, as his army was still in Corassan, determined to collect as many men as he could. Therefore he hastily sent two great generals into the country of Diarbec [Diyar-Bakr], who collected about 20,000 men and marched with them to the fords of the Euphrates. But hearing that Selim was coming in great force, they did not feel strong enough to oppose him, but returned to Coi [Khawi], where there is a wide valley or plain called Calderan [Chaldiran]. Here they halted, and the Sophi joined them in person. While they were here the Turk kept advancing, so that he arrived not far from that place, ravaging and burning all the country he passed through. The Sophi monarch having left for Tauris in order to assemble more troops, the two generals, seeing the enemy approaching so near, determined to attack him. The Turks fought with desperation, as their provisions were failing, and if they had been defeated, all would have perished. On the 23rd of August, therefore, in the year 1514, the first division of the Suffaveans [Safavids] with half the troops began the fight by routing those opposed to them, dispersing and cutting them to pieces. But Sinan Bassa [Pasha] with his troops coming up, many on both sides were killed, and the squadron of Stugiali [an Ottoman general] was defeated, he himself being taken prisoner and his head cut off, which was afterwards sent to the Sophi. At this moment the second division of the Persians came up and fought so valiantly that they put the enemy to flight, so that the Turk was compelled to retire with his whole force to where the Janissaries and the artillery were, his troops being in confusion, but the genius of Sinan Bassa rallied them, and the Suffaveans were routed and all the camp taken, together with one of the Sophi's wives.

12 / THE EFFECT OF FIREARMS ON MIDDLE EAST POLITICS AROUND 1500

The double victory of Sultan Selim, during his short reign of eight years, over the Safavids of Persia and the Mamluks of Egypt, was due, at least in part, to the superior firepower of the Ottoman artillery. It was crucial for the subsequent history of the Middle East, because it set a pattern that was not seriously altered for four centuries, that is, until the time of the First World War. Professor D. Ayalon, of the Hebrew University of Jerusalem, assesses the impact of the new weapons of war, gunpowder and cannon, on Middle East politics at the opening of the sixteenth century.

Firearms, used though they were in the Mamluk kingdom on a very large scale, yet met with total repudiation on the part of the units forming the social and military elite of the army. This fact not only determined the fate of the Mamluk kingdom itself, but also had far-reaching effects on the future of Western Asia and Egypt for many generations to come. For it is inconceivable that the Ottomans, but for their total superiority in firearms, could ever have inflicted such crushing defeats on their two Muslim enemies, the Safawis and the Mamluks, or that they could have annexed and held until the very dismemberment of the Ottoman Empire such vast territories. This conclusion is based on the following arguments:

In 1502, only a few years before the battles of Chaldiran and Marj Babiq, a new and vigorous State was set up in Persia, headed by a great leader (Isma'il as-Safawi) and imbued with the ideal of promoting the cause of the Shi'a and fighting the Sunna both within and without its borders. Such a State in itself constituted a grave challenge to the Sunni Ottoman Empire, and the menace was greatly increased by the fact that Eastern Anatolia was infested with Shi'a adherents. More than that. Isma'il as-Safawi was himself not a Persian but a Turcoman, and he was very greatly venerated and even

From *Gunpower and Firearms in the Mamluk Kingdom* by D. Ayalon, pp. 108-11. Copyright © 1956 by Valentine, Mitchell & Co., Ltd., London. Reprinted with permission of the publishers.

idolized among many Turcoman tribesmen who flocked in their thousands to his standard. Had the Ottomans not put an abrupt and decisive end to this process, their hold on vast areas in the Eastern parts of their realm would have been greatly jeopardized, and the Shi'a doctrine would have registered one of its most resounding successes.

It was perfectly natural therefore that the Ottomans in tackling, their Muslim adversaries, directed their attention first to the East. At Chaldiran (August 1514) Ottoman artillery and arquebuses wrought havoc among the ranks of the Safawis who had no similar arms with which to reply and consequently had forced them to retreat into the interior of the Persian kingdom. The Ottomans conquered vast territories; but they did not succeed in annihilating the Safawis. Had the Ottomans not employed firearms on such a large scale in the battle of Chaldiran and in the battles that followed it, it is reasonably certain that their victory—even if they had been able to win—would have been so far less decisive. In other words, the Ottomans would have acquired far less Safawid territory in that event and a much stronger Safawid army would have been left intact to prepare for a war of revenge. Such a threat on the left flank of the Ottomans, combined with a danger of insurrection among the oppressed Shi'a in Eastern Anatolia, would have greatly diminished the chances of an Ottoman offensive against the Mamluks. The Ottomans could proceed to deal with the Mamluks only after they had succeeded, by the liberal use of firearms, in rendering the Safawis powerless for many years to come.

The Mamluk army, despite its internal dissensions and despite the process of deterioration it underwent, was still a formidable opponent for any army equipped with weapons similar to its own. . . . Had the Ottomans fought them with bow, lance and sword, it is doubtful whether they could ever have been beaten at all. The evidence proves beyond any shadow of doubt that by far the most important cause of Mamluk defeat was the Ottoman use of firearms.

In planning the conquest of the territories lying to the east and south of their Empire, the Ottomans had to reckon not only with the power of their two Muslim rivals, but also and to an even greater extent with the situation on their main front in Europe.

The Ottomans could embark on great campaigns, absorbing the bulk of their armed strength, in the east and south when there was a long lull on their north-west front—but not otherwise. Such a lull did indeed occur when Sultan Selim launched his offensives against the Safawids and the Mamluks. But Selim, owing to his superiority in firearms, could count on a blitzkrieg—and hence on the early return of his main forces to his main front.

Even according to the most reserved and conservative estimates, the wars against the Safawids and the Mamluks would have been much more protracted if the Ottomans had employed the traditional weapons. Under such circumstances, would an Ottoman Sultan have dared expose his north-west frontier through wars in Asia and Egypt which perforce would have lasted very long? Even if at the outset there had been good prospects of a long peace on the European front, would not an Ottoman Sultan have shrunk from the possibility of a Christian attack while his main armies got bogged down in a series of indecisive battles on the Muslim front? For the Christians would not have allowed such a golden opportunity for attack to slip by. Moreover, communication and means of transport within the Ottoman Empire were notoriously bad, and a determined enemy could achieve great successes before the Sultan found time to rush adequate reinforcements from an area lying perhaps many hundreds of miles away.

Thus the combined effect of the Safawis, Mamluks, the European front and bad communications, but for the effective use of firearms, would have rendered the Ottoman conquests of the early sixteenth century most unlikely. It follows that firearms were a most decisive factor in shaping the destinies of Western Asia and Egypt for four centuries (1517-1918), for had this area not been incorporated in the Ottoman Empire, its history would have been entirely different.

IV / MAMLUK EGYPT

INTRODUCTION

For more than 250 years (1250-1517) Mamluk Egypt was one of the Muslim Great Powers. A strange ruling class of ex-slaves (*mamluk*, white slave, as distinct from *abd*, black slave) governed the submissive Egyptians and the less submissive Syrians. Most of the Mamluks came originally from the Turkish-speaking Kipchak people of south Russia, later from the Circassian tribes of the Caucasus. These slaves were commonly transported from their homelands via the Genoese colonies on the Black Sea coasts and Constantinople; on arrival in Cairo they were sorted out and trained for positions in either the civil or the military establishment. The ablest of them rose to be governors, generals, ministers, and the sultanate itself was within their grasp. The Mamluk government was essentially a permanent military dictatorship; the sultan, himself an ex-slave, was an absolute monarch, but hereditary succession was not favored, and his son was rarely allowed to succeed to the throne.

The Mamluks rendered important services to Islam. They defeated the Mongols and expelled the Crusaders, and they made Cairo into a second Baghdad, the last home of the old Arabic learning. When the Mongols in 1258 sacked Baghdad and killed the last caliph to exercise sovereign power there, the Mamluks installed a relative of the murdered prince as a puppet caliph in Cairo, and, as custodians of a shadow line of caliphs, they won additional prestige among their coreligionists.

They succumbed in the end to the double pressure of the Ottomans in the north and the Portuguese in the south and were thus

49

the first important political casualty of the European intrusion into the Indian Ocean. The native Egyptian chroniclers attribute their fall, however, to the arrogance and misgovernment of the Circassians, who despised and oppressed the other Mamluks.

13 / THE CHARACTER OF MAMLUK RULE

The nature of Mamluk rule and in particular the unsatisfactory relations between the Turkish and Circassian ruling class and the Egyptian-Arab masses, which partly explain why the regime, having no popular backing, collapsed so ignominiously before the blows of the Ottomans in 1516-17, are here analyzed by an American scholar.

The Mamelukes were white slaves, either captured in war or bought while children. Most of them came from the Caucasus and Asia Minor, especially Circassia. Originally a bodyguard to the kings of Egypt, they eventually became so strong that in 1250 they seized power and elected their own monarch to the throne. They continued this practice of choosing their emperor [sic] from their own number and passing over the last one's sons, for it was a rule with them that their children should retain only their deceased parents' property and should forfeit whatever offices they held. In Egypt the Mamelukes were brought up as soldiers. Varying from 10,000 to 16,000 in number, they were successful in maintaining their rule over the people of Egypt and Syria because the Mamelukes held together as a single people when danger confronted them, and were intensely loyal to their owner and his descendants even after generations. Their rule was really an oligarchy in that whenever the necessity arose they would assert supremacy over their Sultan and his courtiers. . . . Although they held the Empire with no danger of serious revolt, their rule was not popular, and their subsequent defeat by the Turks was not regarded by the Arabs as a national misfortune.

The Arab dislike of the Mamelukes was based on suspicion and distrust of foreigners whom the Arabs could neither understand nor converse with. The Mamelukes rarely spoke Arabic, preferring to

"The Ottoman Turks and the Arabs" by G. W. F. Stripling. From *Illinois Studies in the Social Sciences,* pp. 17-21. Copyright 1942 by the University of Illinois Press. Reprinted with permission of the publisher.

use Circassian. Furthermore, the Mamelukes were clannish; although they themselves were divided into many factions, each with a leader or patron, they would still unite against the common people. They did not intermarry with the natives, except very rarely. In spite of the fact that they were very well paid, receiving six *ashrafi* or ducats ($15) per month besides maintenance for themselves and their horses and families, they were very oppressive to the people. Vast wealth was extracted from the subjects of the Empire, and rich fiefs were obtained from the central government. In an effort to make them pay more to the rulers, peasants and townspeople were beaten mercilessly. The populace could neither bear arms nor ride horses or mules unless in the presence of the Mamelukes. In fact, a traveller of the sixteenth century said the Arabs lived under the Mamelukes like the lamb under the wolf. . . . If a Mameluke killed an Arab in a dispute, there would be no one to censure him. If the Arab were not killed, he could be deprived of a hand or an eye or basti- nadoed if he dared strike the Mameluke in self-defence. Though killings were probably not very common, an Arab knew that if he failed to get out of the way of a Mameluke quickly enough, or jostled him in passing, or did not greet him obsequiously enough, the Mameluke could beat him as much as he chose. Not even a father or son could venture to help his child or sire when under- going such punishment. Even women were not safe from their rulers, who could attack them with impunity, even daring to enter their houses at high noon and drive out the victim's family in order to fulfill their desire.

Not only did the Mamelukes receive high salaries, but also they were exempt from the frequent and heavy customs duties. Besides, on the death of a sultan, they expected to receive as an outright gift from 100 to 200 ducats apiece. Not satisfied with this, the Mame- lukes were very disorderly on such occasions, for they seized the opportunity of the lack of a ruler to extort money from the un- protected populace. Since the average reign of the Egyptian sultans under the Mameluke regime was less than six years, the rule of this body of men cost the Empire very much, especially because the Mamelukes, knowing that on the death of their sovereign they would get more pay, were thus constantly tempted by the prospect of a revolt. . . .

Men of letters were encouraged by the Mamelukes, who made the period of their rule the Saturnian age of Moslem Egyptian art and literature. Some of the greatest authorities in Moslem theology, jurisprudence, criticism and history were associated as cadis (judges) or professors with the mosques and medressas (schools) of Cairo. The Sultans produced or encouraged the talent of Ibn Khaldun, Nuwairi, Ibn Duknak, Makrizi, Ibn Hagar, al-Aini, Ibn Arabshah, Abu-l-Mahasin, Es-Suyuti and Ibn Iyas, who were either born in Egypt or like Abu-l-Fida, spent many years in Cairo. The fifteenth century perhaps was the most prolific period in Egyptian literature, and this activity was more than rivalled in the neighbouring province of Syria under the same Sultans.

14 / AN EGYPTIAN CHRONICLER DESCRIBES THE OTTOMAN DEFEAT OF THE MAMLUKS, 1516

The last effective ruler of Mamluk Egypt was Kansuh al-Ghuri (1501-16), who was an elderly man of over sixty at his accession. His rule is depicted by the chroniclers as harsh and tyrannical; he increased the taxes, debased the currency, and shocked the pious by raiding the revenues of the wakfs, *or religious foundations, in a vain effort to replenish the treasury. He was, however, in many respects the victim of circumstance. The Egyptian economy had long been declining, and the revenues of the state suffered accordingly. The opening up of the Cape route to India by the Portuguese in 1497-98 dealt a staggering blow to Egyptian trade; in 1507 for the first time, we are told, no Indian wares of any sort reached Cairo. Notwithstanding Ghuri's threat to destroy the Christian holy places in Jerusalem if the Portuguese did not stop attacking Muslim shipping in the Indian Ocean, the aggressive Europeans appeared in 1506 in the Red Sea and the Egyptian fleet was beaten off Diu in 1509 and had to retire, bruised, to its bases. Egyptian merchant vessels had to run an increasingly stringent blockade, the Indian trade dwindled to a trickle, the Mamluk state verged on bankruptcy, the soldiery were unpaid, and popular discontent grew.*

In these conditions, it was unwise for the aged Sultan to involve himself in the bitter feud between the Ottomans and the Safavids, but it was perhaps inevitable. Since the Ottoman conquest of southeast Asia Minor, the Turks and Mamluks had a common frontier and clashes between them became frequent. In Cairo the growth of Ottoman power was viewed with mounting uneasiness, and, though the rise of Shah Isma'il was at first highly displeasing to Sultan Ghuri, a loyal Sunnite, the latter soon came to feel that a successful challenge by the Safavids to the Turks would be to the advantage of the Mamluks. When Selim attacked Isma'il in 1514, Ghuri moved his main force to Aleppo in north Syria, taking with him the Abbasid caliph, and offered his services as an intermediary. Selim was unsure of his intentions and dared not pursue Isma'il into the heart of Persia after the battle of Chaldiran lest his exposed flank be attacked from Syria by the Mamluks. Once certain the Safavids had been so severely beaten that they would pose no threat for some time, Selim resolved to make an end of the Mamluk threat. The two Powers clashed over disputed territory in Mesopotamia; Ghuri was charged with intriguing with the heretics; war broke out; the Ottomans invaded Syria; and at Marj Dabik near Aleppo, in August 1516, the fate of the Near East was decided for four centuries. The Mamluks, though as valorous as ever, were no match for the Ottoman artillery; the old Sultan disappeared in the melee, his body being never found, and the caliph fell into the hands of the enemy. In Cairo, when the news of the disaster was received, the chief amirs raised to the throne one of Ghuri's relatives, Tuman Bey, who was given little chance to save the falling state. Selim marched rapidly through Palestine into the Nile valley; the remnants of the Mamluk forces were routed at Raidaniya outside Cairo (January 1517); and Tuman Bey fled up the river, whither he was pursued by the conquerors. Selim offered to make peace on condition that his suzerainty was recognized and his name put on the coins. The offer was rejected and the Ottoman envoys killed. This criminal folly sealed Tuman Bey's fate; he was captured, brought back to Cairo, and hanged from one of the city gates. Egypt became a province of the Ottoman Empire.

A vivid picture of the battle of Marj Dabik and the death of Sultan Ghuri is given by the Egyptian chronicler Ibn Iyas, who died about 1521 and who is thus a contemporary witness.

[The Sultan] proceeded to Merj Dabek . . . [where] he was suddenly surprised by the presence of a body of troops of Shah Selim Ibn Othman. . . . He mounted his charger, wearing a light turban and mantle, carrying an axe on his shoulder; he inspected the army

From *The Ottoman Conquest of Egypt, 1516* by Ibn Iyas. English trans., pp. 41-44, 58-61. Copyright 1921 by Royal Asiatic Society, London. Reprinted with permission of the publisher.

in person; on the right wing was the Amir of the Faithful [the caliph], also wearing a light turban and mantle, carrying an axe on his shoulder like the Sultan, and having over his head the Khalifah's [caliph's] banner. Around the Sultan, borne on the heads of a body of nobles, were forty copies of the Koran in yellow silk cases. . . . There were also around him a body of dervishes. . . . The Royal Red Standard was carried about twenty yards behind the Sultan, and under it marched the chiefs of the Memlooks [Mamluks].

At first the army of Egypt was victorious; would that it had continued so! [The battle turned in favour of the Ottomans.] Now the Sultan was standing under the flag with a small body of Memlooks, and he began to call out: "Oh, sirs, now is the time to quit yourselves like men, this is the time to show your valour." But none listened to him, and they began to leave him, whilst he told the Fakirs to pray to God for victory, "for now," he said, "your prayers are needed." But no help or succour came. The Sultan's heart became as a redhot coal, which could not be extinguished. The day, too, was fiercely hot, and such a dust was raised between the opposing armies that they could scarcely see each other. God's anger was kindled against the Egyptian troops, and their hands seemed to be fettered, so that they could not fight. . . .

Now as the confusion and terror increased, Amir Tamr feared for the safety of the Sultan's standard, so he lowered it, folded it up and concealed it. Then he approached the Sultan and said to him: "Our King and Master, the troops of Ibn Othman are upon us, save thyself and go back to Aleppo." When the Sultan understood this, a kind of paralysis fell upon him, which affected one side, and caused his jaw to drop. He asked for water, and they brought him some in a golden cup, from which he drank a little. Then intending flight, he turned his horse round, moved a few paces, fell off his horse, stood for a moment, and died from the effect of his defeat. It was said that his gall-bladder burst, and that red blood flowed from his throat.

When his death became known, Ibn Othman's troops advanced against the men who were round the Sultan; they killed Amir Baibars, one of the Commanders, and a number of the bodyguard and of the Sultan's servants. As to the Sultan, his body was not found amongst the dead, nor was it ever known what became of it; it was as if the earth had swallowed it up there and then. Therein is a lesson to him who considers. . . .

Thus the rule of al-Ghuri came to an end, in the twinkling of an eye, as though he had never been. Praise be to Him Whose kingdom never wanes and Who never changes!

He died at about the age of seventy-eight, having reigned over Egypt and Syria for fifteen years, nine months and twenty-five days, every day of which seemed to the people a thousand years. . . . He was tall, bulky and big-bellied, fair complexion[ed], round-faced, sleek-eyed and loud-voiced. . . . He was unthwarted until he and Selim Shah, Emperor of Constantinople, quarrelled, and he went out to meet him, and such a tragedy happened as never happened to any other King of Egypt. Amongst the Sultan's virtues it may be said that he was good-natured, controlled his temper, and considering his strong passions was not over-violent. He understood poetry and was fond of instrumental music and singing. He was not excitable. He was very fond of reading history and travels, and collections of poetry. He was affable, liked joking and jesting in his company; though rough-looking he was amiable and civil by nature— contrary to the Turkish character. . . .

Adulteration of the coinage went on all through his reign . . . [and] the affairs of the country steadily deteriorated. Damascus and Aleppo also declined; he used to make them liable for large sums of money every year, and they in turn would wring the money from their peasant subjects. . . . Husein, Deputy of Jeddah, used to lay a tax of 10% on the goods of Indian merchants so they gave up coming to the port of Jeddah, and its prosperity declined. There was a scarcity of cotton-stuffs in Egypt, and also of goods imported from Europe, of rice and leather; the ports of Alexandria and Damietta similarly declined, European merchants refusing to enter them owing to the extortions practised there. He placed an impost on the sale of corn, and even put an embargo on salt. . . . No important trader escaped this system of extortion. . . . His avarice increased to such an extent that he wrung from the small cultivators a share of the profits they made from the cow-dung collected out of the gutters.

V / ISLAM IN THE EURASIAN STEPPES

INTRODUCTION

Ever since the tenth century Islam had made headway among the nomadic or seminomadic tribes of Turkish speech who lived in the vast steppelands stretching from south Russia to Mongolia. In the thirteenth century all these regions and many others became part of the Mongol world empire created by Chingiz (Jenghiz) Khan. The most westerly part came to be known to the Russians as the "Khan-ate of the Golden Horde," whose ruling dynasty was descended from Chingiz's grandson Batu, the conqueror of Russia. "Horde" is the Europeanized form of *ordu,* a Turco-Mongol word meaning "camp." The center of this khanate was in the lower Volga, and its capital at Saray, sixty-five miles north of Astrakhan. The ruling house was pagan Mongol, but the population was a mixture of Turks, Finns, and Russians. As the Turks mostly belonged to the Kipchak confederacy of tribes, the title "Kipchak Khanate" is often given to the Golden Horde. The direct rule of the khans extended as far west as the Crimea and as far east as Turkestan. The Russian princes were their vassals for nearly two hundred years and had to come regularly to Saray to pay tribute and do homage to the khan. The Horde, like the Mongols everywhere, encouraged commerce and in particular did a brisk trade in slaves from the Caucasus tribes and elsewhere, who were sold mainly to the Mamluks of Egypt. This brought it into close connection with the Muslim lands of the south; Islamic influences seeped in, and the Khan Ozbeg, or Uzbek, who reigned from 1313 to 1341, embraced the faith of Muhammad. The Horde thus became a Muslim Power, and the

Turkish element came to predominate. Conversion to Islam imposed a permanent barrier between the Horde and Russia, which grew increasingly conscious of her role of defender of Orthodox Christendom against Muslim expansion into Eastern Europe. Yet the political impact of the Horde on Russia was strong and lasting. The Russians addressed the khan as "Tsar," meaning "Emperor" or "Supreme Ruler"; he in turn charged the Grand Duke of Muscovy with collecting the tribute, and the Tsardom of Muscovy later arose on the model of the khanate, the title being transferred to the Grand Duke. An autocracy, unlimited by law or representative assemblies or corporate bodies, grew up in post-Mongol Russia, and set the pattern of Russian politics for centuries.

The power of the Horde dwindled in the fourteenth century. Strife over the succession to the khanate weakened it; the rise of the Ottoman Turks checked its expansion toward the Mediterranean, and the growth of Muscovy and Poland-Lithuania (united since 1369) threatened its western frontiers. In 1380 the Russians beat a Horde army for the first time at Kulikovo ("the Field of Curlews") on the Don. Shortly afterward the Horde's territories were invaded and devastated by the mighty Timur (Tamerlane), who sacked Saray in 1395, and the unity of the state was destroyed by the emergence of separate khanates in Kazan, Astrakhan, and the Crimea, which last came under the protection of the Ottoman Turks in 1475. As late as 1480, however, the Horde was still strong enough to threaten Moscow, but Ivan III's successful resistance finally broke its power. In 1502 its line of khans came to an end, and its territory was divided between the Russians and the smaller khanates. Of the latter, Kazan and Astrakhan fell to Russia in the mid-sixteenth century, thus opening the path to Russian expansion beyond the Volga and the Urals into Siberia: the Krim (Crimean) Khanate, shielded by Ottoman naval power in the Black Sea, survived down to 1783.

The fall of the Golden Horde had important repercussions in the heart of Asia, where it contributed to the rise of the last great nomadic empire of the steppes, the Uzbek. Batu granted his brother Shaiban a large tract of land east of the Golden Horde, between the Irghiz River and the Urals and extending from the upper Tobolsk in the north to the Jaxartes and lower Chu in the south. The Blue

Horde, as Shaiban's descendants were known, later adopted the name Uzbek, apparently from the Golden Horde khan of that name, who accepted Islam. They emerged as a strong power during the long reign of Abu'l-Khair (1428-68), who skilfully exploited the family squabbles of the heirs of Timur and got control of territories in Khwarizm and the Jaxartes valley. His grandson Shabani Khan (1500-1510) fought both the Safavids of Persia and their ally Babur, the future conqueror of India, and made the Uzbeks masters of Transoxiana and Khurasan and the great cities of Bukhara and Samarkand. As Transoxiana was always strongly Sunnite, Shabani was cast for the role of defender of orthodoxy in Eastern Islam against the heretical Safavids and as such he received encouragement from the Ottoman Sultan Bayezid II.

The Uzbek empire lasted over a century, coming to an end in 1599. Ruled by descendants of Chingiz Khan, it controlled in its heyday the steppes of western Turkestan and the settled, urbanized region of Transoxiana, the breakup of the Golden Horde having enabled the Uzbeks to some extent to supplant it. But the Uzbeks failed to stop the advance of Russia into Asia or to penetrate Persia and overthrow the Safavids. The last great agglomeration of power made by Turco-Mongol nomads, they rose to prominence at a time when new military techniques and the widespread employment of firearms were destined to end forever the day of the mounted archer. The Portuguese, who wished to prop up the Safavid regime as a counterweight to the Ottomans, supplied Shah Isma'il with cannon and muskets to fight the Uzbeks, which he did successfully, Shabani being killed near Merv in 1510. The high cost of importing firearms (which they could not manufacture themselves) into Turkestan effectively weakened the military power of the nomads; by 1600 the ascendancy of the armed horseman of the steppes was gone for good.

15 / AN ITALIAN ENVOY CROSSES THE LAND OF THE GOLDEN HORDE

Venetian missions to Persia multiplied in the fifteenth and sixteenth centuries, the Republic being anxious to build up an alliance against the Ottomans, whose growing navy was imperiling Venice's colonies in the eastern Mediterranean. Some of these missions traveled overland through the territories of the Golden Horde; the

*one which crossed the Volga and the Russian steppes in 1476 has
left a report of conditions there in the last years of the Horde's
supremacy. The reigning khan was Ahmad (c. 1465-81), the last but
one of the successors of Batu, and a crisis was approaching in the
relations between Russia and the Horde. Ivan III, the Grand Duke
of Muscovy, allied himself with the subkhanates of Kazan and the
Crimea and entered into friendly contact with Usun Hasan, the
Turcoman ruler of Persia. Having thus effectively isolated the
Horde, Ivan refused to continue the payment of tribute. Ahmad
demanded that he should come to Saray and explain himself; Ivan
refused; and in 1480 the Khan marched on Moscow, but, afraid of
an attack from the Crimea and overtaken by a severe winter, he
retired without striking a blow. A year later he was killed in battle
with the Shabanids east of the Urals. In 1502 the khan of the Crimea
took Saray, and the Golden Horde vanished from history. From this
time dates the emancipation of Russia from Mongol domination.*

On the 15th [April 1476] the wind springing up in the morning
we made sail, and after coasting those cane islands nearly the
whole time, entered the mouth of the Volga on the 26th. The Volga
is a very large river and deep in many places; it flows from Russia
and discharges itself into the Sea of Baichu [Baku—the Caspian],
it is said by 72 mouths. From its mouth to Citracan [Astrakhan] the
distance is 75 miles. On account of the strong current which we
ascended, sometimes by towing, sometimes by means of the wind,
we did not reach Citracan till the 30th. The Tartars, that is, the
Lord of Citracan, would not allow us to come on shore that day.
Marco was, however, permitted to land, as he had some friends in
the town. On the first evening I also was admitted with my people
into the little house where Marco lodged, and accommodated for
the night. In the morning came three ill-favoured Tartars, who told
Marco that he was welcome, as he was the friend of their lord, but
that for me, I had become his slave, as the Franks were their enemies.
I thought this a strange reception. But Marco answered for me, and
would not allow me to say a word, except to recommend myself
to them. This was on May 1st, 1476. I returned to my little chamber
in such dread, that I scarcely knew where I was; and my perils increased every day, not only in consequence of the Comerchieri

From *Italian Travels to Tana and Persia* ed. C. Grey. The Hakluyt Society,
London, 1873, pp. 149-55. Reprinted with permission of the Hakluyt Society.

[customs officers], who gave out that I had a quantity of jewels, but from having some trifling things I had brought from Derbent and intended exchanging for horses; but everything was taken from us. I was afterwards told by Marco that they intended selling them in the bazaars; but that by interceding with some merchants who were going to Muscovy, he had, with much trouble and risk, and after a delay of several days, arranged that I should pay the sum of 2000 *aleruri* to the lord. This sum did not include what was extorted by others. As I had not a soldo [an Italian coin worth about a half-penny], the money was advanced on very usurious terms by Russian and Tartar merchants who were going to Muscovy, on security given by Marco. Although our difficulty with the lord might be said to have been overcome by this arrangement, the dog of a Comerchiere used to come to our house, when Marco was not at home, and after knocking down my door, would threaten in his cursed voice to have me impaled, saying I had jewels in quantities. I was therefore obliged to appease him as best I could. Many and many a time also Tartars, drunk with a beverage they make with apples, used to come and shout that they would have the Franks, who had not the hearts of men. We were terrified into purchasing their silence also.

We remained at Citracan from May 1st to August 10th, the feast of St. Lawrence. Citracan belongs to three sons of a brother of the present Emperor of those Tartars who inhabit the plains of Circassia and the country lying in the direction of Tana. In the heat of the summer they go towards the confines of Russia in search of fresh pasturage. These three brothers remain in Citracan a few months in the winter, but in the summer do like the rest. Citracan is a small town situated on the Volga, and surrounded by a low wall. The few houses it contains are built of bricks; but it is evident that it possessed several edifices at no very distant period. Citracan is said to have been in ancient times a place of considerable trade, the spices which came to Venice by way of Tana having passed through it; and from what I could understand they were sent direct from Citracan to Tana, a distance of only eight days' journey.

On August 10th, 1476, we left Citracan. The Lord of Citracan, named Casimi Can [Qasim Khan], sends an ambassador to Russia every year to the Duke of Muscovy (more for the sake of obtaining presents than anything else), who is accompanied by a great many

Tartar merchants who form a caravan and take with them silk manufactured in Gesdi and fustian stuffs to exchange for furs, saddles, swords, bridles and other things which they require. And as the country between Citracan and Muscovy is a continual desert, everyone is obliged to carry provisions. The Tartars, however, care little to do so, as they always drive a great number of horses with them, some of which they kill every day for food. They live indeed continually on meat and milk, without other food, no one being even acquainted with bread, unless it be some merchant who has visited Russia. . . . Our way was between two tributaries of the Volga; but as the said emperor was at war with Casimi Can, his nephew—who pretended that he was the true emperor, his father having been the Emperor of the Lordo [i.e., the Horde], and in possession of territory—it was unanimously resolved that the whole caravan should cross over to the other bank of the river and proceed as far as a narrow pass between the Tanais [Don] and the Volga, about five days' journey distant, as beyond that point it might be considered out of danger. . . .

When the time came, [Marco] made me mount on horseback with the ambassador and my interpreter; and with great fear, riding as low as I could, we arrived at the pass, at about an hour before sunset. As I was about to cross the stream, as darkness was coming on, to join our people, Marco called to me in such a furious tone that I certainly thought my last hour had come. He made me mount with my interpreter and a Russian woman, together with a Tartar, whose aspect was as forbidding as could well be imagined. All he said was, "Ride, ride fast." As I could not do otherwise, I obeyed, and followed the Tartar all that night and until midday the next day, nor would he allow me to dismount for a moment. Having asked him several times through my interpreter where he was taking me to, he at length replied that Marco's reason for sending me forward was that the Khan was going to have the boats searched, and he feared that if I were discovered, I should be detained. This was on August 13, about midday. Having come to the river, the Tartar tried to find a boat wherewith to cross over to a little island, where there were some cattle belonging to the ambassador Ancholi. Not finding one, he collected some branches, which he bound together as well as he could, and after placing the saddles on them, tied them with a rope to the tail of a horse, which he drove to the island, a distance, I should think, of two good bowshots. He then returned and took the Russian woman, whom he passed over in the same way. My interpreter preferred to swim over, which he did with some peril. He then came over for me, and as I saw how great the danger was, I took off my shirt and hose, although in this case, this would have availed me little; and by the help of our Lord, although in great danger, I was carried over. The Tartar then returned again, and brought over the horses, which we mounted, and proceeded to his lodging—a skin covering—which I got under. This was the third day I had not eaten, and when he gave me a little sour milk, I received it with the greatest thanks, and thought it very good. Shortly afterwards, there came a number of Tartars, who were on the island minding their cattle. They looked at me, and appeared to wonder much, amongst themselves, as to how I had come there, as no Christian had ever been there before. . . . I remained there until the 16th, when Marco arrived with the caravan. . . . We remained the whole day of the 17th, and then started with the caravan to cross the desert on our way to Muscovy. The ambassador took the command of the whole company which with Russians and Tartars might have amounted to about 300 persons. There were besides more than 200 horses led for food and for sale in Russia. We certainly marched in good order, keeping by the side of the river, sleeping at night and resting at midday. We proceeded thus for fifteen days, during which time they no longer appeared apprehensive of the Emperor of the Lordo, as they were before reaching the narrow pass. This Lordo is governed by an emperor, whose name I do not remember, who rules over all the Tartars in these parts. [This was Ahmad, who was Khan of the Golden Horde from about 1465 to 1481.] These Tartars as I have said are constantly wandering in search of fresh pasturage and water, and live entirely on meat and milk. They have, I believe, the most beautiful oxen, cows and sheep in the world, the meat being of good flavour on account of the excellence of the pastures. Mare's milk, however, is held in great estimation. Their country consists of beautiful and extensive plains, where not a mountain is to be seen. I did not visit this Lordo myself, but was desirous of obtaining what information I could respecting it and its numerical strength. It is the general opinion that although it contains a great many people, one thousand men armed with sword and bow could scarcely be mustered in it, all the rest being women and children in considerable numbers, or men shoeless and without arms of any kind. They are accounted valiant, as they plunder both Circassians and Russians. Their horses are no better than wild; they are timid, and it is not the custom to shoe them. These Tartars themselves were generally looked upon as brutes. As has been said, they dwell between the rivers Tanais [Don] and Volga. But there is said to be another tribe of Tartars living beyond the Volga, in an east-north-east direction, who are supposed to be very numerous. They wear long hair reaching to their waists, and are called wild Tartars. They wander in search of pasturage and water like the others; and in winter, when there is much cold and ice, they are said to come as far as Citracan; nor do they commit any damage in the town, unless it be pure paltry theft of meat.

16 / THE UZBEKS: SHABANI, THE LAST NOMAD CONQUEROR

This appraisal of Shabani Khan and his Uzbeks is taken from the History of Bokhara *written by the famous nineteenth-century Hungarian traveler and orientalist Arminius Vambéry (1832-1913), who visited and described the countries of Central Asia in the 1860s and '70s on the eve of their annexation by Russia. He noted that Muslim civilization in Turkestan had been stationary since the days of the Uzbeks, who permanently separated the once flourishing land of Transoxiana from the Persian world.*

When the once powerful Golden Horde of Kipchiak had been broken up into four parts, and Ivan III, the deliverer of Russia from the Tartar yoke, was menacing the power of Juji's descendants on the upper course of the Volga, we find the name of Abu'l-Khair, prince of the Uzbegs, in the list of chiefs and vassals who renounced their allegiance to the ruler at Sarai and exercised the rights of sovereignty as "grey beards" or independent khans. Abu'l-Khair had gradually retired with the tents and herds of his nomads, before the

From *History of Bokhara* by A. Vambéry. London, H. S. King, 1873, pp. 245-46, 270-72, 298-99, 302.

storm which was gathering in the north of Christendom against the Muslim power, and had sought refuge in the eastern steppes. . . . The Uzbegs, far removed from the influence of the Mohammadan civilization of the western Sarai and southern Transoxiana, and by nature a rude barbarian people, retained the rough character of the old Turanian warriors much longer than their brethren who had settled down in fixed habitations. . . . They only nominally professed the religion of the Arab Prophet; their habits and customs like themselves were a strange mixture of Turkish-Mongolian elements, and while the Turks on the banks of the Oxus and Yaxartes were gradually becoming familiarized with the language, literature and general refinement of Iran [Persia], the Uzbegs still went about wrapped in sheepskins and horseskins. . . . Later on they settled down by degrees into fixed habitations and gradually threw off their barbarous customs. . . .

Sheibani [Shabani] was the last of the world conquerors who came forward supported by the rude strength of the inhabitants of the steppes of Central Asia and founded an empire extending far beyond the Oxus; after his time, fortune no longer favoured any warrior, whatever his abilities or his talents might have been, to the same extent, and the consolidation of affairs in Iran [Persia] opposed an insurmountable barrier to the extension of the influence of Bokhara and Samarkand to the west. Secondly, the ethnographical revolutions in Central and Western Asia entirely disappear from this time forward, for the Özbegs [Uzbeks] were the last tribe who descended from the *officina gentium* [" 'factory' of peoples"] of the Turanian highlands into the South West. Thirdly, the fall and total extinction of the Timurides destroyed the last though feeble links still binding the Mohammadans beyond the Oxus and the Yaxartes to their brethren in Western Asia. This rupture was naturally hastened by the Shi'ite zeal of the Sefides [Safavids], who drove as it were a wedge into the centre of Islamism. This hierarchical-social revolution was just accomplished when Sheibani descended with his nomads from the northern steppes into the country; the separation of Transoxiana was thus rendered more complete, and the river of the Oxus gradually became again, as it had been in ancient times, the frontier-line dividing Iranian and Turanian life from each other.

As regards the individuality of Sheibani, he most assuredly was not the wild barbarian he is represented by his Iranian enemies. He showed great respect, and even childlike submission to the religious teachers of his time, was himself addicted to the muses, and always carried a small pocket library about with him in all his campaigns. . . . Baber [Babur, the future conqueror of India] says ironically that Sheibani wrote stupid tasteless poetry and had it read publicly; but even this statement proves that this man of the sword, following the notions of culture prevailing in his day, busied himself also with his pen, and he distinguished himself in this way above most of his compeers, for in spite of the sarcastic remarks of his deadly enemy, his compositions bear evidence of remarkable poetic talent and of a thorough acquaintance with the Turkish, Persian and Arabic languages. He took into his service many learned men who were left homeless and destitute and gave them liberal salaries; he built mosques and colleges at Bokhara, Samarkand and Tashkend, and was always accompanied, even in his campaigns, by different learned men, who exercised the greatest influence over him, and although when he first appeared on the scene of history, the name of Özbeg was thought synonymous with rudeness and barbarism, and later, even down to the present day, has still been considered so by the Iranians, this definition does not apply to Sheibani personally.

It will be as well to give some idea of the state of civilization existing during the busy period of the Sheibanides, an epoch during which the process of separation of the east Islamite world from western Islam was completed and Mohammadanism assumed the character in which it is met with up to the present day [1873] between the eastern frontier of Iran and China. There was naturally nothing like the amount of culture existing under the Timurides to be found under the Sheibanides. These rough warriors, who believed in the power of their *Yada teshi* (magic stone) to control the elements, cure diseases and ensure victory in battle, were sincerely devoted to their religion and their priests. In the time of the Mongolian occupation, a few remarkable mollahs, in virtue of their spiritual powers, had been practically rulers of the land, controlling by their veto the will of the most imperious despots, and this experience was repeated under the Sheibanides. The teachers of godly wisdom not only enjoyed the complete devotion of the people, but the princes vied with each other for their favour, and whether we ascribe it to superstition or to fear of popular opinion, it remains equally a most remarkable manifestation, how the mightiest princes of this dynasty invariably bore themselves towards the mollahs, not only with respect but with all the marks of the most abject humility . . . [though this] represents after all a very petty and miserable state compared with the luxury, wealth and civilization reigning at that very time amongst the Sefides in Persia, or with the noble objects pursued at that moment in India by another prince of Turanian origin, Timuride Ekber [Akbar, who was Great Mogul from 1556 to 1605], who founded the great empire on the Indus and the Ganges in which he reigned gloriously and splendidly for a space of fifty years, studying and investigating both Christianity and the doctrines of Bramah, and devoting himself to the welfare of his people.

INTRODUCTION

One of the most spectacular triumphs of Islam in the sixteenth century was the establishment of the Mogul empire in India at the same time that the Europeans were driving Muslim shipping from the Indian Ocean. The Indus valley had been seized by the Arab Muslims as early as the eighth century, and from the time of Mahmud of Ghazna (999-1030), Turkish Muslim chiefs steadily enlarged the sphere of Islam in India by pushing deep into the Gangetic plain as far east as Bengal. A series of Muslim dynasties ruled in northern India, and the Delhi Sultanate, as the principal Muslim state was known, threw off a number of "successor states" including the Sultanate of Gujarat and the Bahmanid kingdom in the Deccan. Thanks to the total lack of any "national" feeling in India and the attraction which Islam exerted on the low castes of Hindu society, who provided the bulk of Muslim converts, no serious organized Hindu resistance was encountered, except in the far south where a strong Hindu kingdom, that of Vijayanagar, maintained itself till 1565.

The last pre-Mogul dynasty to rule in the north was that of the Afghan Lodis, or Tughlaks, who had had to endure Timur's invasion and the sack of Delhi in 1398. Babur, the founder of the Mogul empire, considered himself the heir of Timur, though he had more Turkish than Mongol blood in his veins, and this drew him toward India after the Uzbeks had expelled him from his ancestral lands in Farghana.

Babur's life is well known to us because of his unique auto-

69

biography composed in the Chagatai dialect of Turkish. Born in 1481, he had to fight against the Uzbeks from his boyhood for his inheritance and, to save it, was driven to make an alliance with the Safavids. The defeat and death of Shabani Khan at the hands of Shah Isma'il in 1510 gave him a chance to regain Transoxiana, but the Uzbeks were able to pose as champions of Sunnism against the Shi'ite heretics, Babur (himself a Sunnite) was compromised by his association with the Safavids, and he was finally obliged to relinquish all his territories save that round Kabul. As compensation for this loss, he resolved to carve out for himself a new kingdom in north India and defeated the last Lodi Sultan Ibrahim at Panipat in 1526. This event marked the beginning of Mogul power, which was not, however, finally established till the reign of Babur's grandson Akbar (1556-1605).

The Mogul empire had a Turkish (rather than Mongol) ruling class; it professed Sunni Islam, the embarrassing association with the Safavids being dropped after the conquest, but its language and culture were Persian. There had, in fact, been a considerable migration of Persian officials and men of letters into Muslim India after the Mongol invasions of the thirteenth century, and this was reinforced after 1500 by Persians who were unwilling to accept the new Shi'ite regime. The Safavids were in some respects narrow puritans who discouraged art and literature, with the result that Persian culture found a home in India and encouragement from Babur and his successors.

Though a powerful Sunnite Muslim state was constructed in the north of the Indian subcontinent and ultimately penetrated deep into the south, it did nothing to restore Muslim control of the Indian Ocean, which by the time of the battle of Panipat was firmly in Portuguese hands. The Moguls were landsmen, with little or no understanding of naval matters; the independent Muslim kingdoms of the south, in particular the Bahmanid Sultanate in the Deccan, were equally afraid of the Portuguese and the Moguls and looked for succor at times to the Safavids, at times to the Ottomans. The political disorganization of south India was not overcome till the seventeenth century.

17 / BABUR'S ACCOUNT OF INDIA AND OF HIS VICTORY AT PANIPAT, 1526

Babur's account of the India he conquered has often been quoted. His attitude was that of a devout Muslim Turco-Mongol hillman toward the rich, urbanized, but largely pagan (Hindu) culture of Hindustan with its passive and unwarlike population. He was an acute observer with an unquenchable curiosity, and no more vivid picture exists of the India of the early sixteenth century.

From the date 910 [=A.D. 1504-5] at which the country of Kabul was conquered down to now [A.H. 932 = A.D. 1525-26], my desire for Hindustan had been constant, but owing sometimes to the feeble counsel of begs, a move on Hindustan had not been practicable and its territories had remained unsubdued. At length no such obstacles were left: no beg, great or small, could speak an opposing word. In A.H. 925 [=A.D. 1519] we led an army out and, after taking Bajaur by storm and making a general massacre of its people, went on to Bhira. Bhira we neither overran nor plundered, we imposed a ransom on its people, taking from them in money and goods to the value of four *laks* [1 lak = 100,000 rupees] and having shared this out to the army, returned to Kabul. From then till now we laboriously held tight to Hindustan, five times leading an army into it. The fifth time God the Most High, by His own mercy and favour, made such a foe as Sultan Ibrahim the vanquished and loser, such a realm as Hindustan our conquest and possession.

From the time of the revered Prophet down till now three men from that side [i.e., from north of the Hindu Kush] have conquered and ruled Hindustan. Sultan Mahmud of Ghazna was the first, Sultan Shihat ud-Din the second, I am the third. . . .

The time *we* came to Bhira, we had at most 1500 to 2000 men. Dependent on me were the countries of Badakshan, Qunduz, Kabul and Qandahar, but no remarkable profit came from them, rather it was necessary to reinforce them fully because several lie close to an enemy. Then again all Transoxiana was in the power of the Uzbeg-khans, an ancient foe whose armies counted up to 100,000.

From *Memoirs*, by Babur. English trans. by Mrs. A. S. Beveridge, *The Babur-nama*, vol. 2, pp. 478-84. Copyright 1921 Luzac & Co., London. Reprinted with permission of the publishers.

Moreover, Hindustan from Bhira to Bihar was in the power of the Afghans and in it Sultan Ibrahim was supreme. . . . His army was estimated at 100,000, and people said his elephants and those of his amirs were 1000.

Under such conditions in this strength and having in my rear 100,000 old enemies such as are the Uzbegs, we put trust in God and faced the ruler of such a dense army and of domains so wide. And our trust in Him the Most High God did not make our labour and hardships vain, but defeated the powerful foe and conquered that broad land. . . .

[Hindustan] is a wonderful country. Compared with our countries, it is a different world; its mountains, rivers, jungles and deserts, its towns, its cultivated lands, its animals and plants, its people and their tongues, its rains and its winds, are all different. . . . Most of the inhabitants of Hindustan are pagans. Most Hindus believe in the transmigration of souls. All artisans, wage-earners and officials are Hindus. . . . Hindustan is a land of few charms. Its people have no good looks; of social intercourse, paying and receiving visits, there is none; of genius and capacity none; of manners none; in handicraft and work there is no form or symmetry, method or quality; there are no good horses, dogs, grapes, musk-melons or first-rate fruits, no ice or cold water, no good bread or cooked food in the bazaars, no hot baths, no colleges. . . . Pleasant things of Hindustan are that it is a large country and has masses of gold and silver. Its air in the rains is very fine. . . . Another good thing in Hindustan is that it has unnumbered and endless workmen of every kind. There is a fixed caste for every sort of work.

The battle of Panipat, which gave the Ganges valley to the Moguls, was fought in the same year as that of Mohacs, which gave most of Hungary to the Ottoman Turks. Babur mentions that he adopted the Ottoman device of placing his matchlockmen behind a barrier of carts, a practice that, it is claimed, the Turks borrowed from the Hussite armies of Ziska in Bohemia in the fifteenth century. A cavalry charge could be broken up when the horsemen got entangled in the carts and the ropes or chains linking them together.

At our next camp it was ordered that every man in the army should collect carts, each one according to his circumstances. Seven

From *Memoirs,* by Babur, pp. 468-75.

hundred carts were brought in. . . . The order given was that these carts should be joined together in Ottoman fashion, but using ropes of raw hide instead of chains, and that behind every two carts five or six mantelets should be fixed, behind which the matchlockmen were to stand to fire. When everything was ready . . . we marched forward, halted one night on the way, and reached Panipat on [April 12, 1526]. . . . During [the] seven or eight days we lay in Panipat our men used to go a few together close up to Ibrahim's camp, rain arrows down on his massed troops, cut off and bring in heads. On [April 20] news came that the enemy was advancing in fighting-array. . . . Our right, left and centre and turning-parties having surrounded the enemy, rained arrows down on him and fought ungrudgingly. He made one or two small charges on our right and left but, under our men's arrows, fell back on his own centre. When the incitement to battle had come, the sun was spear high; till midday fighting had been in full force; noon passed, the foe was crushed in defeat, our friends rejoicing and gay. By God's mercy and kindness, this difficult affair was made easy for us. In one half-day that armed mass was laid upon the earth . . . [and] it was afternoon prayer when Tahir Tibri, who had found Ibrahim's body in a heap of slain, brought in his head.

18 / THE CHARACTER AND ACHIEVEMENT OF BABUR

Babur's character is sketched and the nature of his government analysed by an able and industrious Anglo-Indian historian of the early nineteenth century, William Erskine (1773-1851), from whose History of India under Baber and Humayun *the following extract is taken.*

Baber was certainly one of the most illustrious sovereigns that ever filled an eastern throne. His character was happily compounded of most of the qualities that go to form a great prince and a good man. He was bold, enterprising, full of ardour, and possessed of the commanding talents that sway and lead the minds of men. His temper was frank, confiding, and gay, and maintained through life the freshness of youth. He had strong affections, the warmest do-

From *History of India under Baber and Humayun,* by W. Erskine. London, 1854, vol. 1, pp. 519-30.

mestic feelings, was devotedly attached to his relations and friendly and ready to sympathise with the pleasures and sufferings of human beings of every class. Keenly alive to whatever was grand or beautiful, he cultivated knowledge of every kind with unwearied assiduity and with proportional success. Glory in every shape inflamed his imagination, and he attained to a rare eminence of power and renown. Yet no man's success could be more entirely his own. When as a boy he mounted the throne of Ferghana, the neighbouring kingdoms were all held by sultans and sovereigns of his own race. While he was still only a youth, not one of them was left; they had all either fallen by domestic treason, or been swept away by foreign invasion, the torrent of which overwhelmed him also, and bore him into distant lands; but by his native energy, he emerged from the sweeping inundation, and raised himself above it, the only remnant of the House of Timur. Before the age of twenty he had experienced every diversity of fortune, having been by turns a petty prince, the conqueror of a renowned kingdom, and a houseless and hunted fugitive; but under no circumstances did his sanguine temper, and his determined resolution, forsake him; and when in the lowest pitch of misery, expelled from his hereditary dominions, and wandering with a few ragged followers, the fame of his valour brought to his standard many thousand bold adventurers, aided by whom he conquered new and extensive kingdoms. In that age of confusion, to be able to reign it was necessary to be a soldier; and he became the first of his time.

His fondness for war did not lead him to neglect the arts of peace. The few intervals of repose from military operations which he enjoyed in his troubled life, he devoted with his habitual ardour, to examining into and improving the state of his kingdom and to bettering the condition of his subjects. His natural genius made him fond of all the fine arts, and among others of architecture and gardening. He built palaces and laid out gardens in several parts of his dominions; he delighted in flowers and beautiful prospects. He was a horticulturist and succeeded in naturalising some valuable fruits and plants in provinces to which they had formerly been strangers, and where they still flourish; and was as proud of his success as of a victory in the field of battle. All this he did in the midst of the turmoil of war. In the course of his most important expeditions, we find him inquiring after the progress of his improvements and expressing an earnest longing to be restored to the scenes and friends that he loved. It is not surprising that with so inherent a love of knowledge he should have been a patron of learning and of learned men; that by his liberality he should have drawn many of them around him; but the fact that in a life so full of agitation and bustle as his, he having from boyhood to age been in constant motion, he should himself have found time to cultivate the learning and knowledge of the age, is a proof how strong was the natural bias of his mind to useful and liberal studies. "He was," says Haidar Mirza, who knew him well, "a prince adorned with various excellences and distinguished for his admirable qualities. Of all these qualities his generosity and humanity took the lead. In Turki poetry none equalled him. He has composed a Turki Diwan (or collection of odes) of extreme elegance and vigour. He wrote a useful treatise on Law and Religion, which has met with general approbation. He also composed a tract on Turki prosody, superior in merit to any written before on the subject. His Commentaries [Memoirs], which he composed in Turki, are remarkable for their easy and unaffected manner and great purity of style. He was also skilled in music and other arts. None of his family before him exceeded him in talents and accomplishments; and in wonderful exploits and adventures, none of his descendants is soon likely to equal him."

No part of his character is more admirable than his uniform humanity and kindliness of disposition. If in the course of his Memoirs some cruel executions appear, they belong to the age, not to the man. The historians of his reign remark that whenever any either of his nobles or brothers had revolted, or entered into cabals against him, no sooner did they acknowledge their offence and return to their duty than, to use the words of Khafi Khan, "contrary to the custom of the princes of Persia, Arabia or India, he not only forgave them but never retained towards them any feeling of resentment."

In stature he is represented as having been above the middle size; he was of great vigour of body, fond of field sports, and athletic exercises, a skilful archer, and an excellent swordsman. On numerous occasions he distinguished himself by his prowess; in several instances by engaging and slaying his adversary hand to hand in single combat. Such indeed was his bodily strength that he is said at times to have run along the battlements of a fort, having a man under each arm, and though thus encumbered, to have kept on, leaping over the embrasures that he met in his way. . . .

The dominions of Baber at the time of his death were very extensive, stretching from the river Amu to Behar. Beyond the Hindu Kush range he possessed Badakhshan, with Kunduz; and all the districts to the south of the Oxus, as low down as the borders of Balkh. To the south of the mountains he had the kingdoms of Kabul, Ghazni and Kandahar, and much of the mountainous country of the Hindu Kush and Ghuri ranges, inhabited by Afghans, Aimaks and other tribes, some of them migratory; as well as the hilly and desert tracts to the south as far as the borders of Baluchistan, in all of which the tribes, though self-governed, acknowledged his authority. To the east of Ghazi and Kabul, below the passes, the lowlands of Jilalabad, Peshawar, the Kohdaman, as well as Swad and Bajour, and in general the more extensive and cultivated plains or accessible country had submitted; but over a great portion of what we now designate Afghanistan, especially the more inaccessible hills and secluded valleys, his sway was hardly admitted by the rude tribes that traversed them; and prudence was satisfied with some easy acknowledgment which was treated as tribute. Occasional inroads were made into the territories of such as were refractory, or offered tempting booty in cattle or other property; they on their part infested the roads, plundered the merchants or caravans, drove off the flocks, or carried away the harvests of their neighbours in the lower grounds. In Upper and Lower Sind the khutba was read in his name; but although his supremacy was acknowledged, he had little direct power. To the east of the Indus all the Punjab, including Multan—and to the south and east of the Satlej the rich provinces of Hindustan lying between that river and Behar on the one side, and the Himalaya mountains and the countries of the Rajputs and of Malwa on the other—were subject to him; the western boundary being nearly a line marked by the fortresses of Biema, Rantanbor, Gwalior and Chanderi. On the south towards Bengal the limits of his authority are not well defined. Though he possessed the greater part of Behar, some portions of it, especially the hilly or wooded parts of the country, were still held by the remains of the Afghans or by native chiefs. On the frontier of his empire, the Rajput principalities, the shattered kingdoms of Malwa, Bandelkand and Bengal were still independent states; though the language of overweening superiority used by Indian authors who treat even foreign war as a rebellion, might often betray an incautious reader into the erroneous conclusion that they were subject to Delhi.

There was little uniformity in the political situation of the different parts of this vast empire. Hardly any law could be regarded as universal, but that of the unrestrained power of the prince. Each kingdom, each province, each district, and (we may almost say) each village, was governed in ordinary matters by its peculiar customs. There were no regular courts of law spread over the kingdom for the administration of justice. Such disputes as occurred in the Hindu parts of the country were settled by the village or district officers of the vicinity, or by a kind of conventional arbitration, subject to an irregular appeal or complaint to the superior chief or governor. Where Musulmans were concerned, though the Kazi [cadi, kadi] was nominally a judge, his active jurisdiction appears to have been chiefly confined in practice to cases of marriage and divorce, claims arising out of marriage contracts, and to questions considered as properly religious. All differences relating to land, where they were not settled by the village officers, were decided by the district authorities, the collectors, the zemindars and jagirdars.* The higher officers of government exercised not only civil but criminal jurisdiction, even in capital cases, with little form and under little restraint.

We have very imperfect means of knowing what were the taxes then levied. The chief revenue of the state has always been in India a kind of landtax, which in the fully settled and quiet provinces was raised directly on the land; but when the country remained under its native chiefs or was not fully subdued, was drawn by the Emperor in the shape of an annual tribute.

The rights of landed property were considerably different from those that prevail in the west. There were two separate and legal

* Zemindars and jagirdars were landholders, the former usually State tenants, the latter possessors of estates granted to them as a reward for public service.

rights in the land; that of the ryot or cultivator, who held it by hereditary succession; and that of the government, which could justly claim a fixed share of the produce. Both of these were permanent.

We frequently see the officers of the army or government rewarded by jagirs or estates. But these jagirs were not like our territorial possessions or landed estates in Europe. Though the larger ones implied a jurisdiction both civil and criminal, very much resembling that enjoyed by the greater feudal chiefs during the middle ages, or by barons holding of the crown in Scotland down to the abolition of the hereditary jurisdictions in the last century [i.e., after the Jacobite rising of 1745], yet their legal power over the land itself did not extend to a property in the soil, but to the exercise of all such rights as belonged to the government; for instance, that of levying the government's share of the produce and the government taxes. Though the Musulman conquerors claimed in theory an absolute right of property in the soil, the right was in practice restrained in conformity with the ancient law and usage, to some fixed position of the produce collected from villages or small zemindars or separate ryots [peasants]. Their exactions were indeed often oppressively increased, but the ryot was rarely removed; and he considered the land as his by right, subject to the payment of a certain share of the produce, varying according to circumstances. The jagirdar or holder of the jagir was properly in Musulman times merely an officer of government and removable at pleasure, except where the grant had been made hereditary. The term zemindar or landholder is applied by Musulman writers not only to persons who held lands granted by the crown but even to the great Hindu chiefs and rajas, who had possessed their lands unrestricted from the remotest times; though the more powerful of these chiefs considered themselves as of right independent, and yielded obedience not to a law, the existence of which they denied, but to fear or the pressure of a superior force. India in reality was rather a congeries of little states under one prince, than one regular and uniformly-governed kingdom. Many of the hill and frontier districts yielded little more than a nominal submission.

Besides the landtax there were other sources of revenue. There was a duty levied on the frontier on goods imported by caravan or otherwise. The tangha or stamp was the mark by which on cattle and on goods the payment of duties was ascertained. There were transit duties on merchandise transported from one part of the country to another; there was a shop tax, chiefly in towns; and in those parts of the country where the Muhammedans had a confirmed and safe ascendancy, the jezia or poll-tax was levied on all who were not Musulmen.

It may be remarked that Baber was the first prince who ordered all his marches to be regularly measured, as well as his journeys and hunting excursions; an operation which must have tended to improve the geography of a country then very imperfectly surveyed. He also established a regular series of post-houses from Agra to Kabul, at a distance of about fifteen miles from each other, and stationed relays of six horses and proper officials at each.

19 / A COMPARISON OF THE OTTOMAN AND MOGUL EMPIRES

The two Muslim Great Powers of the sixteenth century ruled over large non-Muslim minorities, Balkan Christians in the case of the Ottomans, Hindus and Sikhs in the case of the Moguls. Both were Sunnite, but were separated throughout their history by Shi'ite Persia, though Persian culture was influential in Istanbul as well as in Delhi and Agra. Persian was the official language of the Mogul court to the end, and Urdu, the common speech and literary language of Muslim India, was written in the Arabic script and its vocabulary was filled with Persian words. The following selection by the American historian, A. H. Lybyer, provides an illuminating comparison and contrast between the Ottoman and Mogul empires.

The Mogul emperors perhaps never ruled so large a territory as the Ottoman sultans, but their lands were far more productive; moreover, having from five to ten times as many subjects as their Western cousins and an income in proportion, they could surpass even the Magnificent Suleiman in display and largesse. . . .

The Moguls shared with the Ottomans their relation to the ideas of the Mongol and Turkish Tartars of the steppelands, and to

From *The Government of the Ottoman Empire* by A. H. Lybyer, Appendix IV, pp. 278-304. Copyright 1913 by the Harvard University Press. Reprinted by permission of the publisher.

those of the Persians and Arabs. They were more directly and vitally influenced by the Tartars and Persians, and less directly by the Arabs. Farther than this their relations were not to the comparatively organized and energetic civilization of the Mediterranean but to the more speculative and passive culture of India. Over the lands into which they entered as conquerors lay the shadow not of sternly practical Roman legalism, but of Hindu and Buddhist contempt for things mundane.

They founded a despotism but one that was never so closely related to the Sacred Law of Mohammed as was the government of Suleiman. They ruled a variety of lands in a variety of relationships, but never with the stern control exercised by the Kaisar-i-Rum (Roman Emperor), the name which they gave to the Turkish ruler at Constantinople. They enforced the obedience of many peoples, who spoke many languages and practised many forms of religion; yet they never held these peoples under any such iron system of subjection as that which dominated the Christian subjects of the sultan, even to the seizure of their children for tribute. . . . The institutional structure of the Mogul Empire was decidedly inferior to that of the Ottoman Empire in solidity, system and persistent energy.

The family life of the house of Babur was more normal than that of the house of Osman. In contrast with an almost unbroken line of Ottoman slave mothers and wives, whose names with those of their daughters have hardly survived, many of the Mogul imperial ladies are well known. . . . Turki princesses, ladies of high Persian descent, and daughters of Hindu Rajahs, were taken into the imperial harem, where no emperors sprang from slave mothers during the period of greatness. With such a policy in the family which constituted a chief element in the unity of the Mogul Empire, it was but natural that officers and soldiers, statesmen and public servants, should be accepted with a like catholicity. The best fighters, of course, continued to be those who came down newly from the high country beyond the North West passes; and since such of those as met success were apt to send for relations and friends, there was continual recruiting from among Tatars, Persians, Afghans and Arabs—all Moslem, but of various sects. "Rumis" from the Ottoman Empire were especially useful in the artillery service.

Some of them were doubtless European renegades, but "Firingis" or Franks were likely to come more directly from Portugal and other European countries. Yet by no means all the brave were from foreign lands. Many Rajputs under their own Rajahs served the Mogul emperors most acceptably, and when treated without prejudice they were faithful. The high officers of government were usually Persian; about one in eight of [Akbar's] paid cavalry chiefs was a Hindu; and of the lesser civil service positions the mere necessity for numbers, apart from superior skill and training, required that many should be held by Hindus.

When the Ottoman Turks conquered their European territories, as well as parts of their Asiatic dominions, they for the first time introduced the Moslem religion. This was not the case with the Mogul advance into India . . . [as] when Babur came, there remained little of India that was not actually or had not at some time been under Moslem rule. . . . In the absence of an elaborate slave system in India, there was not the steady public machinery of conversion which operated powerfully in the Ottoman Empire. . . . For a century the government lent little encouragement to change of faith. Down to the accession of Aurangzeb [1658], there was a clear contrast between the Ottoman and Mogul policy in the attitude towards the Moslem religion: the Moguls held far less than the Ottomans to the idea of the conquest of the world for Islam, or to the conversion of unbelievers, as an object of governmental endeavour. . . .

The succession to the Mogul throne never became regular, since neither by Mongol nor by Moslem custom was any one method prescribed. Nor did the more kindly disposition of the house of Babur ever permit the publication of such a decree as that of Mohammed II for the execution of brothers upon the accession of a sovereign. Accordingly, the resources of the empire were apt to be wasted in civil wars between father and son, and between the older and younger brothers. The Ottoman method was more practical if less humane. . . .

As the army was the defence and prop of the Mogul government, so finance was its sustenance. Akbar reduced to order and regularity the existing revenue system, which in the course of centuries of varying rule had become much confused. By ancient custom of

India, the sovereign as primary owner of the land was entitled to one-third of the crops in kind. It was Akbar's task to change the system to a more modern money regime, a step in progress which the Ottomans have not been able to take to this day [1913]. India, importing less of other commodities than she exported, steadily absorbed gold and silver. It is likely that a large share of the wealth of the newly-discovered Americas had already by Akbar's day made its way to India through the increasing Portuguese trade, and that Columbus, Cortes and Pizarro thus unwittingly gave him the means of modernizing his land revenue.

In comparison with conditions in the Ottoman Empire, Moslem and non-Moslem in the India of the early Moguls were far more nearly on a level. This was due not merely to the tolerance and indifference of the emperors, but even more to the circumstances of the conquest, under which both groups were treated alike, since Babur at Panipat in 1526 subdued the Moslem Lodi Sultans of Delhi, and at Kanwaha in 1527 the Hindu Rajput confederacy. Indian-born worshippers of Allah and of Brahma, Vishnu and Siva were mingled in the same vast mass of conquered subjects, equally separated from the victorious invaders. . . . Suleiman was distinctly the head of the Moslems in his empire. Through his appointee, the Sheik ul-Islam, and other learned and saintly personages, he kept in close touch with the religious chiefs of the Mohammedan population. All who prayed towards Mecca, at least from the older parts of the Ottoman Empire, were attached by many ancient ties to the house of Osman. No such vital bonds joined to the Moguls the great mass of their Moslem subjects. These remembered the glories and favours of lost dynasties, and were indebted to the new sovereigns only for defeats and humiliations which depressed them towards the level of the Hindus, whom they had for centuries held to be far inferior to themselves. They had no *Sheik ul-Islam,* honoured by the sovereign with a seat above his own, whose decisions might determine the fate of the ruler or of the empire. Almost as much to them as to the Hindus the emperor was a stranger and a foreigner, to whom should be rendered because of his power full submission and instant obedience, but not loyal affection and whole-hearted devotion.

VII / ISLAM IN SOUTHEAST ASIA

INTRODUCTION

Nowhere during the century 1450-1550 was the expansion of Islam more rapid and remarkable than in Indonesia and Malaya. The process is badly documented: The impulse is not altogether clear, nor the reasons for the decline and fall of Hindu culture in the Archipelago. Two extracts are quoted here, one, a kind of official Muslim account of the propagation and acceptance of Islam in a Hindu-dominated Malay state, the other, a modern European scholar's analysis of social and religious conditions there at the turn of the fifteenth and sixteenth centuries, which favored the success of a new (or at least an outside) faith. It has been argued that the coming of the Portuguese encouraged conversion to Islam rather than to Christianity because the local rulers saw in it a source of unity and strength against the European intruders. It is noteworthy that Islam, though it penetrated China from the landward side and gained a strong footing in Kansuh, never made any impact on coastal China or succeeded in repeating in the Philippines or Japan its success in Malaya and Indonesia.

20 / A HINDU RAJA ACCEPTS ISLAM

This extract, from a Muslim Malayan chronicle, provides evidence that Islam's missionaries in these parts were Arab traders; indeed, the connection between Java and the Hadramawt in southern Arabia has always been close.

In the annals of Queda, one of the northernmost of the states of the Malay peninsula, we have a curious account of the introduction

From *The Preaching of Islam* by T. W. Arnold. Luzac & Co., London, 1896, pp. 373-74.

of Islam into this kingdom about A.D. 1501, which is as follows: "A learned Arab, by name Shaikh Abd Allah, having come to Queda, visited the Raja and inquired what was the religion of the country. 'My religion,' replied the Raja, 'and that of all my subjects is that which has been handed down to us by the people of old. We all worship idols.' 'Then has your Highness never heard of Islam and the Koran which descended from God to Muhammad, and has superseded all other religions, leaving them in possession of the devil?' 'I pray you, then, if this be true,' said the Raja, 'to instruct and enlighten us in this new faith.' In a transport of holy fervour at this request, Shaikh Abd Allah embraced the Raja and then instructed him in the creed. Persuaded by his teaching, the Raja sent for all his jars of spirits (to which he was much addicted), and with his own hands emptied them on the ground. After this he had all the idols of the palace brought out; the idols of gold and silver and clay and wood were all heaped up in his presence, and were all broken and cut to pieces by Shaikh Abd Allah with his sword and axe, and the fragments consumed in fire. . . . The Raja sent for his four aged ministers, who on entering the hall were surprised to see a Shaikh seated near the Raja. The Raja explained to them the object of the Shaikh's coming, whereupon the four chiefs expressed their readiness to follow the example of his highness. . . . Shaikh Abd Allah said to the four ministers, 'What is the name of your prince?' They replied, 'His name is Pra Ong Mahawangsa.' 'Let us change it for one in the language of Islam,' said the Shaikh. After some consultation the name of the Raja was changed at his request to Sultan Muzlaf al-Shah, because the Shaikh averred, [']it is a celebrated name and is found in the Koran.' ['']

21 / THE COMING OF ISLAM TO SOUTHEAST ASIA

A leading British authority on the history of Southeast Asia, drawing on the specialist work of Dutch orientalists, gives an acute analysis of the causes favoring the introduction and spread of Islam in a former Hindu "colonial" area. The process began with the conversion of the ruler of Malacca.

Malacca gave a new impetus to the propagation of Islam in South-East Asia. The first Muslim ruler of Pahang was a son of the Sultan of Malacca. When he died in 1475 his grave was marked by a stone inscribed in classical Arabic. . . . Trengganu officially adopted Islam on becoming a vassal state of Malacca. Patani was converted from Malacca; Kelantan as Patani's vassal. A Muslim prince is mentioned as ruler of Kedah in 1474. Across the Straits Roka entered the Islamic fold in the first half of the century, Kampan, Indrigiri and Siak later. Brunei also, the first Muslim state to appear in Borneo, came to accept Islam through its trading connections with Malacca. The Malacca dynasty saw in Islam a political instrument of great potential value; by adopting the religion officially it secured admittance to "the unity of Islam" with its assurance of powerful allies, and its expansive ardour. Thus as Malacca established overlordship over the states of the peninsula and of the east coast of Sumatra across the Straits, so Islam penetrated them. It was a political weapon against Buddhist Siam; still more it supplied the Malaccan empire with a cohesive force which enabled it to hold together after the Portuguese capture of Malacca itself. . . . Malacca received not only its spices but also its vital food supply through the east Javanese ports. The trade was in Javanese hands and by the beginning of the sixteenth century they formed the most important element in Malacca's population. Its army was Javanese; most of the shipwrights were Javanese, and the great Javanese aristocratic families who ran the trade between eastern Indonesia and Malacca were represented there. In this way was Islam introduced into the coastal districts of Java, which were asserting their independence of the declining empire of Majapahit, to become a potent weapon in their struggle against the Hindu-Buddhist central authority.

One of van Leur's most interesting theories was that the propagation of Islam in Indonesia received its strongest impetus from the appearance of the Portuguese in the Indian Ocean in 1497. . . . "The race with Christianity" had actually begun before the arrival of the Portuguese in the East. The close coherence of the Muslim powers found expression in their annual meeting at Mecca, and through this medium rumours of the Christian struggle against Islam in the Iberian Peninsula reached Indonesia ahead of the Portuguese. Hence by the time of their arrival the Muslim powers were already pressing on to extend Islam's influence as widely as possible. When Malacca fell in 1511 to the Portuguese, and became a strategic centre for their attack upon Islam and the Islamic trade in the vast island world of South-East Asia, the Crescent was already a move or two ahead of the Cross. It never lost its lead. The Muslim traders, driven out of Malacca, settled in the rising north Sumatran state of Acheh, which by the middle of the sixteenth century became the most important entrepôt for the trade of the Indian and West Asian Muslims with the Archipelago, and like Malacca and its predecessor Pasai, a centre of Islamic studies.

If our knowledge of the spread of Islam in South-East Asia as a political force is far from adequate, even more so is the picture that can be presented of its progress as a missionary movement. Scholars are generally agreed that the trader was the most common missionary. Throughout the area where Islam spread, the ruler was the chief merchant, he controlled all essential trade and traders, for he directed and controlled all supplies of the basic commodities required by them, rice on Java and in Macassar to exchange for spices in the Spice Islands, pepper at Bantam and the ports of south-east and south-west Sumatra, pepper also and especially gold at Acheh. He had the first choice of all the goods brought to his country, bought them wholesale at his own prices, and fixed the prices at which they were to be sold in the common market. His most important official in dealing with foreign merchants was the Shahbandar (Ruler of the Port), who by reason of his duties was in most cases a foreigner.

Schreike has drawn attention to the important fact that when trade with the Red Sea ports via Cambay and Aden had got into the hands of Muslim merchants after the end of the thirteenth century, foreign Muslims tended to become Shahbandars in the ports both of India and the Archipelago. He suggests that it was through them that Islam extended its influence at court level; they were able to indicate what was considered good form at the great Mohammedan courts abroad, to warn of the danger of Portuguese expansion, and to recommend the adoption of Islam as a means of extending the ruler's own power. They also introduced Muslim scholars and holy men to stimulate his religious zeal and establish centres in his country for Islamic propaganda. The courts became to a greater or less degree centres of Islamic learning, producing a not inconsiderable literature much of which is still extant. . . . In Sumatra and Java brotherhoods of Sufi mystics from India, organized in trade gilds, became an important element in society . . . [and] the Sufi brotherhoods succeeded in spreading Islam because of their tendency to tolerate popular usages and beliefs not in accordance with the strict practice of Muslim orthodoxy. So far as Java was concerned, C. C. Berg sums up what happened as Islamization, not conversion. Most significant of all perhaps is the fact that Muslim law has not the same sanction in Malaya and Indonesia as in other Muslim countries as their own *adat* (customary law) has maintained its position.

The Muslim scholars and holy men played an important part in political as well as religious affairs at the various courts which received them. They both gave impetus to the political expansion of Islam and also strove to promote a sense of unity among the Muslim communities of the Peninsula and Archipelago in opposing the advance of Portuguese and later Dutch power.

VIII / ISLAM IN NEGRO AFRICA

INTRODUCTION

Islam spread early along the caravan routes from Barbary across the Sahara to the Negro lands of the Niger region. Two largely Islamized Negro kingdoms grew up in the late Middle Ages, Songhai in the northern bend of the Niger with its capital at Gao, and Mali in the upper Niger. The former was ruled by a line of chiefs called *sonni,* or "liberator," the last of whom, Ali Ber ("Ali the Great"), who reigned from 1464 to 1492, greatly increased the power of Songhai and captured Timbuktu in 1468. The native chroniclers speak of him as an able warrior, but an impious libertine, only nominally Muslim, and say he was drowned in a torrent in 1492. His best general, Muhammad Ture, then seized the throne, taking the title of *askia,* or "supplanter," and founded a dynasty which lasted down to the fall of the Songhai kingdom on the capture of Gao by the Moroccans in 1591. Muhammad Ture was the most famous Negro empire builder who had appeared up to that time and was clearly a man of high intelligence. In a long reign of thirty-five years (1493-1528), he extended his kingdom from lower Senegal in the west to Bornu near Lake Chad in the east, thereby controlling most of the western Sudan. He created a disciplined standing army, a fleet on the Niger, and a workable administrative system. A pious Muslim, unlike his predecessor, he made the pilgrimage to Mecca in 1497-98 and secured a diploma of investiture, confirming his sovereignty, from the puppet Abbasid caliph in Cairo. His profession of Islam and faithful fulfillment of its precepts undoubtedly strengthened his power. He made Timbuktu an intellectual as well as a commercial center by founding schools there and patronizing scholars. The fame of the city dates from his time. Every encouragement was given to trade, and Barbary merchants frequenting the markets of Songhai brought cloth and horses from Europe into the kingdom, which attained a high level of prosperity. Forced by his sons to abdicate in old age in 1528, he died in 1531, leaving the reputation of a wise, strong, and enlightened prince and a founder of African Muslim culture.

Our knowledge of the great *askia* and of African Islam in general at this time is derived almost wholly from the *History and Description of Africa* by Leo Africanus, one of the most remarkable scholars and travelers of the age, who forms a curious link between the Muslim world and Renaissance Europe. Born al-Hasan al-Wazzan, he was brought up at Fez in Morocco, then a notable seat of Muslim learning, and in 1510, as a young man of twenty or so, accompanied his uncle on a diplomatic mission to Songhai, during which he traveled all over the *askia*'s extensive dominions, carefully observing and recording. In 1518 he was dispatched on an embassy to Sultan Selim; on his way back his ship was caught by a Christian patrol off Tunisia, but his captors, impressed by his accomplishments, took him to Rome and presented him to Pope Leo X, who, seeing the man was a scholar, freed him and offered him a pensioned post at the papal court on condition that he adopt Christianity. He made little difficulty, was baptized with the Pope's name, and was henceforth known as "Leo the African." He learned Italian and wrote up in that language the notes he had made in Arabic during his journey through Songhai, completing the work in 1526. His subsequent career is obscure, but he seems to have contrived to return to Barbary, where he reverted to Islam. He died at Tunis about 1552. The Italian text of his history was published in 1550 and by 1600 had been translated into the leading languages of Europe, including English; the Arabic original has never come to light.

Leo's book was Europe's principal authority on the history and geography of Africa for three hundred years, until the continent was at last thrown open to Western exploration in the nineteenth century. It is vivid, racy, and colorful, and, though by no means free from inaccuracies (he says the Niger flows westward into the Atlantic), it contains a wealth of information given by no other source on what may be called the "African hinterland" of Islam. The following extract, which contains a lively picture of the conquests and rule of the "Izchia" (askia), is taken from the Hakluyt Society's reprint of the old Elizabethan translation of Leo made by John Pory in 1600. Leo saw Timbuktu in the days of its greatest prosperity and helped to create its legend as a place remote, mysterious, and splendid. The European explorers who rediscovered it in the nineteenth century, when it had long sunk into decay, were disappointed at its mean and drab appearance.

22 / THE MUSLIM NEGRO KINGDOMS OF AFRICA AROUND 1500

Our ancient chroniclers of Africa knew nothing of the land of the Negroes. But in the year of the Hegira 380 [= A.D. 990-91], by means of a certain Muhammadan who came into Barbary, the residue of the said land was found out, being as then inhabited by great numbers of people, who lived a brutish and savage life, without any king, governor, commonwealth, or knowledge of husbandry. Clad they were in the skins of beasts, neither had they any peculiar wives: in the daytime they kept their cattle; and when night came they resorted ten or twelve both men and women into one cottage together, using hairy skins instead of beds, and each man choosing his leman [wife, mistress] which he had most fancy to. War they wage against no other nation, nor yet are desirous to travel out of their own country. Some of them perform great adoration unto the sun rising: others worship the fire, and some others approach near unto the Christian faith. . . .

The King of Tombuto [Timbuktu] that now reigns, called Abuacre Izchia [Abu Bakr Askia, i.e., Muhammad Ture], is a Negro by birth; this Abuacre after the decease of the former king, who was a Libyan born, slew all his sons, and usurped the kingdom. And having by wars for the space of fifteen years conquered many large dominions, he then concluded a league with all nations, and went on pilgrimage to Mecca, in which journey he consumed his treasure, that he was constrained to borrow great sums of money of other

From Description of Africa by Leo Africanus. From the Eng. trans. of John Pory in 1600, reprinted by the Hakluyt Society, London, 1896, vol. 3, pp. 819-31. Reprinted with permission of the Hakluyt Society.

princes. Moreover, the fifteen kingdoms of Negroes known to us are all situated upon the river of Niger, and upon other rivers which fall thereinto. And all the land of Negroes stands between two vast deserts, for on the one side lies the main desert between Numidia and it, which extends itself unto this very land: and the south side thereof adjoins upon another desert, which stretches from thence to the main Ocean: in which desert are infinite nations unknown to us, both by reason of the huge distance of place, and also in regard of the diversity of languages and religions. They have no traffic at all with our people, but we have heard oftentimes of their traffic with the inhabitants of the Ocean sea shore. . . .

In the kingdom [of Mali] there is a large and ample village containing to the number of 6000 or more families, and called Mali, whereof the whole kingdom is so named. And here the king has his place of residence. This region itself yields great abundance of corn, flesh and cotton. Here are many artificers and merchants in all places: and yet the king honorably entertains all strangers. The inhabitants are rich, and have plenty of wares. Here are great store of temples [mosques?], priests and professors, which professors read their lectures only in the temples, because they have no colleges at all. The people of this region excel all other Negroes in wit, civility and industry: and were the first that embraced the law of Muhammad. At length Izchia [the *askia*] subdued the prince of this region, and made him tributary [in 1501]. . . .

In Tombuto there is a most stately temple [mosque] to be seen, the walls whereof are made of stone and lime; and a princely palace also built by a most excellent workman of Granada. Here are many shops of artificers and merchants, and especially such as weave linen and cotton cloth. And hither do the Barbary merchants bring cloth of Europe. . . . The rich King of Tombuto has many plates and sceptres of gold, some whereof weigh 1300 pounds: and he keeps a magnificent and well furnished court. When he travels anywhere he rides upon a camel, which is led by some of his noblemen; and so he does likewise when he goes to war, and all his soldiers ride upon horses. Whosoever will speak unto this king must first fall down before his feet, and then taking up earth must sprinkle it upon his own head and shoulders: which custom is ordinarily observed by them that never saluted the king before, or come as ambassadors from other princes. He always has 3000 horsemen, and a great number of footmen that shoot poisoned arrows attending upon him. They have often skirmishes with those that refuse to pay tribute, and so many as they take, they sell unto the merchants of Tombuto. . . . He [the king] so deadly hates all Jews, that he will not admit any into his city: and whatsoever Barbary merchants he understands have any dealings with the Jews, he causes their goods to be confiscated. Here are great stores of doctors, judges, priests and other learned men, that are bountifully maintained at the king's cost and charges. And hitherto are brought divers manuscripts or written books out of Barbary, which are sold for more money than any other merchandise. . . .

The great town of Gago [Gao, capital of the Songhai kingdom, now in the Republic of Mali] being unwalled also, is distant southwards of Tombuto almost 400 miles, and inclines somewhat to the south-east. The houses thereof are but mean, except those wherein the king and his courtiers remain. Here are exceeding rich merchants: and hitherto continually resort great store of Negroes who buy cloth here brought out of Barbary and Europe. . . . It is a wonder to see what plenty of merchandise is daily brought hither, and how costly and sumptuous all things be. Horses bought in Europe for ten ducats are here sold again for forty and sometimes fifty ducats apiece. There is not any cloth of Europe so coarse which will not here be sold for four ducats an ell, and if it be anything fine, they will give fifteen ducats for an ell: and an ell of the scarlet of Venice or of Turkey-cloth is here worth thirty ducats. . . .

The great province of Cano [Kano] stands eastwards of the river Niger almost 500 miles . . . ; the inhabitants are rich merchants and most civil people. Their king was in times past of great puissance, and had mighty troops of horsemen at his command; but he has since been constrained to pay tribute unto the kings of Zegzeg [modern Soso] and Casena [Kasena]. Afterwards Izchia the King of Tombuto feigning friendship unto the two aforesaid kings treacherously slew them both. And then he waged war against the King of Cano, whom after a long siege he took, and compelled him to marry one of his daughters, restoring him again to his kingdom, conditionally that he should pay unto him a third part of all his tribute, and the said King of Tombuto has some of his courtiers perpetually residing at Cano for the receipt thereof. Casena, bordering eastwards upon the kingdom last described, is full of mountains and dry fields; . . . the inhabitants are extremely black, having great noses and blubber lips: . . . a king they had in times past whom the aforesaid Izchia slew, since whose death they have all been tributary to Izchia. . . . The inhabitants [of the kingdom of Zegzeg] are rich and have great traffic unto other nations; . . . they had a king of their own in times past, who being slain my Izchia, they have ever since been subject to the same Izchia.

IX / THE NAVAL STRUGGLE
BETWEEN CHRISTENDOM AND ISLAM

INTRODUCTION

The European Age of Discovery was also the age of a bitter and prolonged struggle between Western Christendom and Islam on the seas and oceans. This was sustained on the Muslim side almost wholly by the Ottoman Turks. Neither the Safavids nor the Moguls were naval powers or ever came to be such. The Mamluks indeed had a fleet, though they found its maintenance difficult as they had to import all the timber they required for shipbuilding; but their state was destroyed by their Ottoman rivals in 1517, and the burden of fighting the Spaniards in the Mediterranean and the Portuguese in the Red Sea and the Indian Ocean fell to the Turkish sultans.

The Ottomans, though a race of landsmen to whom the sea was a strange and unfamiliar element, had early established their power on the Aegean coast of Asia Minor and recognized the importance of a naval arm. They saw that Byzantine Constantinople could not be taken without a fleet, and they hired Christian "renegades" (Greeks, Venetians, Genoese) to build ships for them. When Constantinople fell to them in 1453, they gained possession of its great dockyards and arsenals and rapidly built up one of the world's most powerful navies.

23 / THE OTTOMAN NAVY

The character, training, and armament of the Ottoman navy is here sketched by a British student of Turkish history.

When Suleiman the son of Orkhon first crossed the Dardanelles to make a permanent settlement on European soil, he destined his successors, as a condition of any future greatness, to lay hold on a weapon as yet strange to their hands, a navy. Some of the forts of the Turkish emirates on the south and west coasts of Asia Minor were indeed already nests of corsairs and sea-ghazis; but this scarcely represents a serious use of seapower, which in the case of the Ottomans was an essential strategic and political factor. . . .

For a time the Straits formed a naval cross-roads, the normal— and mainly commercial—traffic between Europe, Constantinople and the Black Sea passing up and down, and the main military and official Turkish traffic crossing principally at Gallipoli. But the balance shifted when Mehmed (Muhammad) II became master of the great dockyards of the capital and was further titled by his seizure of Kaffa and other ports and the general extension of Ottoman control in the Black Sea. Hitherto, the Dardanelles crossing had been at the mercy of the European powers, in theory at least. In future the converse was true, and a great branch of European traffic and intercouse was at the mercy of the Sultan. Henceforth Ottoman seapower contributed to the growth and aggressive policy of the empire and was called on to operate in ever wider areas, being developed in order to protect Turkish trade and communications generally against corsairs Moslem and Christian, and especially stimulated by the recurrent wars with Venice.

It has often been observed that the use of Italian sea terms in the Ottoman navy shows that its technique was a borrowed one: as indeed might be expected, since the Osmanlis were a branch of a race whose background was the purely terrene one of the great Euro-Asiatic steppe. It has less often been pointed out that the geographical destiny which led them as conquerors to the shores of the Aegean and gave them Constantinople as their base, at the same time brought them acquainted with a maritime technique so highly specialized to local conditions as to be unsuitable for use elsewhere, and therefore of limited value to a power aspiring to activities on a more than Mediterranean scale. The bustling sea-world of the

Aegean and Levantine waters upon which the Turks gradually adventured was a very ancient one. Restricted and island-strewn, with a marked type of climate and with seasonal calms and winds that for small early craft decisively limited the safe sailing season, it had developed, 2000 years before their appearance, a nautical skill that was as peculiar to itself and as inappropriate to wider waters as, for example, that which came to perfection on the monsoon coasts. Winter voyages were eschewed: as the Greeks said, those who stayed at sea when the Pleiads sank, sank with them; but in summer the Mediterranean was lively with traffic in all the varied products of the surrounding shores, with pilgrim ships both Christian and Muslim, and with corsairs preying on all this floating wealth.

By the fourteenth century two main types of vessel were to be encountered. Merchantmen were of the "round" type, clumsy sailing ships designed for maximum cargo-space, though not incapable of their own defence. Some of these were already affected by a different ship-building tradition, that of the Atlantic shores, which was to prove itself more flexible and capable of great developments. Very different was the "long ship" or galley, the true Mediterranean fighting-ship built for speed and manoeuverability at the expense of sea-worthiness and sea-endurance, the most efficient "ship-killer" (as distinct from man-killers) that the sea knew before the days of steam power and high explosive. These, built for the sultans by Greek or Genoese or Venetian-trained shipwrights on long-perfected models, were propelled by some 250 rowers, and manned in addition by soldiers and enough mariners to handle the great lateen sail on the single mast, by which in light breezes the rowers' energies were conserved for spurts of speed or for battle. The enormous requirements in manpower of a galley fleet, and the consequent diffculty of carrying enough food and water—fuel for the human engines—for more than a very short voyage, limited its strategic range; but tactically it was a very fine fighting instrument and as such appealed to the Turkish military genius.

From Byzantium the Ottomans took over by degrees huge resources in ship-building materials in the neighbouring lands—timber, tar and pitch, tallow, sailcloth, cordage—as well as much technical skill among their subjects. But the question of motive-power was always crucial, and linked the fleet very closely to the empire's military achievements. Rowers were supplied partly by conscription, and there were a few volunteers, but the bulk were captives taken in war, or seized by the fleet itself as it coasted hostile territory, with frequent halts for watering.

The sufferings of the galley-slaves—cold, naked, chained, working beneath the lash in indescribably crowded conditions that made them an easy prey to epidemics—were long proverbial, even in this country [England], but they were not peculiar to the Turkish service, nor was the danger in battle from rowers whose sympathies lay with the enemy. But the sultans took over the whole long established system as it stood, and under their rule we find all the customs and traditions of the ancient sea-world carried on, from the battle tactics of ramming or boarding and entering, and ceremonial saluting on the grand scale by music, gunfire when that became available, and dressing ship, to such seamen's superstitions as conjuring waterspouts by "crossing" them with a knife.

24 / CAIRO RECEIVES THE NEWS OF THE FALL OF CONSTANTINOPLE

The capture of Constantinople in 1453 was one of the first successes of Ottoman naval policy and put the Turks in a position to deal more firmly with the Genoese and Venetians, who had colonies and trading stations all over the Aegean and Black Sea areas. Muslims everywhere rejoiced in this striking achievement. The following extract, from a contemporary Egyptian historian, describes the reaction in Mamluk Cairo.

There arrived in Egypt the ambassador of Emperor Muhammad Bak [Bey] ibn Murad Bak ibn Uthman, ruler of Asia Minor, to congratulate the Sultan on his rulership, and also to report that with which God had favoured him, in the conquest of the city of Constantinople, which he had taken by force, after a mighty battle, on Tuesday 1 Jamada 20, 857 [May 29, 1453]; they had besieged it from Friday 1 Rabi 26 of this year [April 6] until they took it on the date mentioned. I say: to God be thanks and acknowledgment for this mighty victory.

From *History of Egypt, 1382-1469* by Taghri-Birdi. Translated by William Popper, pp. 38-39. Copyright © 1960 by the University of California Press. Reprinted with permission of the publishers.

With the ambassador had come two prisoners from among the great personages of Constantinople, people of Qustantiniya, the greatest church of Constantinople, and he took them up to the Sultan.

The Sultan and all the men rejoiced at this mighty conquest; the good news was sounded by the bands each morning and Cairo was decorated for it for days. Then the ambassador with the two prisoners before him, went up to the Citadel on Monday Shawwal 25 [October 29], after he and his companions had crossed through the streets of Cairo; people had celebrated by decorating the shops and houses most extravagantly. The Sultan held the court service in the Royal Park of the Citadel of the Mountain. We have recounted the ascent of the ambassador at greater length than this in another passage of our works; in brief, there was a momentous affair at the arrival of the ambassador with the good news; and the Sultan immediately designated Emir Yarshbai al-Mali al-Mu'ayyadi, former second emir of the horse, to go to Ibn Uthman [Sultan Muhammad II] with the ambassador to take the Sultan's reply.

25 / ROME RECEIVES THE NEWS OF THE FALL OF GRANADA

Less than forty years after the fall of Constantinople, the Christian world had a partial revenge: Granada, the last Muslim outpost in Spain, fell to the armies of Ferdinand and Isabella in 1492, and Islam no longer had any footing in Western Europe. The Spanish Muslims in desperation had sent an embassy to Constantinople to beseech the help of the Sultan Bayezid, who is said to have responded by sending a naval squadron to the western Mediterranean, but his intervention failed to save Granada. In any case, he was precluded from pursuing a vigorous policy of aggression toward the Christian Powers, because his brother Prince Jem was in enemy hands. Jem had tried to seize the Ottoman throne, had been defeated, and forced to flee to Rhodes, where he was placed in honorable captivity by the Knights of St. John, who controlled the island and who afterward handed him over to the Pope. He was lodged in a palace in Rome and of course kept under strict guard. He was a hostage for the Sultan's good behavior until his death at Naples in 1495. A prisoner in Rome when the news of the fall of Granada reached there, he had the mortification of being a spectator, or at least a hearer, of the rejoicings and celebrations in the papal city. A biography of him by a modern French scholar gives an account of the scenes in Rome on this occasion, which marked the end of Muslim power in Spain after nearly eight hundred years.

Jem-Sultan was always the object of a strict surveillance. The news of the taking of Granada, the last possession of his co-religionists in Spain, reached Rome on January 31st [1492], [and] was to cause him a profound sadness, intensified further by the ardent demonstrations which in Rome greeted the victory of the King and Queen of Spain. On Saturday February 4th, the great bell of the Capitol rang its full peal, and the Vatican, where Jem, closely guarded, was left to his sombre reflections, was illuminated as well as the Castle of St. Angelo and a great number of palaces and town houses. The next day, Sunday, a procession of all the regular and secular clergy made its way under the leadership of the vicar of Rome from the Basilica of St. Peter's to the Church of the Hospital of St. John of Galicia. After a banquet, the Cardinal Vice-Chancellor Rodrigo Borgia [who in a few months' time was to be elected Pope as Alexander VI] gave in the court of his palace and in the street where he had had an arena built, a bull-fight with five bulls, who were dispatched only after wounding and killing several men. The Spanish ambassadors had had erected in the Piazza di Agome a castle of wood and another behind the Spanish church in order to give a dramatic representation of the capture of Granada and Santa Fé. The show was a wonderful success with the spectators. Next they staged a bull-fight, but apart from a horse being disembowelled, there was no accident. On the following days, the Spanish prelates gave bulls to be killed in public; at the same time, during several days, they organized tourneys in a circus set up for this purpose; Cardinal St. George, Raphael Riario, provided a joust with the lance which lasted a full month, with a prize for the victor consisting of a silver helmet to the value of 200 ducats. But the spectacle which would have affected Prince Jem most was that of the triumph which formed the climax of these festivities. On a chariot drawn by four white horses were seated two personages representing the King and Queen of Spain, a golden palm in their hands and the

From *Djem-Sultan* by L. Thuasne, pp. 293-96. Paris, Leroux, 1892. Translated by the editor.

Moorish king Abu abd-Allah chained at their feet; around them were hung arches, helmets, buckles, shields, lances and swords, as one sees in the ancient triumphs shown on the monuments of the Caesars. Foot-soldiers with gleaming arms led the procession, and in front of the chariot strode chained captives who by their dress and colour gave the illusion of real Moors. Behind the chariot rode cavaliers magnificently clothed and covered with splendid accoutrements. The crowd broke into cheers at the appearance of "Ferdinand" and "Isabella" whose indomitable courage allowed Christian ears, habituated for fourteen years to hearing only news of defeats, to be charmed at last by the announcement of so glorious a victory.

26 / OTTOMAN INTEREST IN AMERICA: THE "COLUMBUS MAP"

The fall of Granada inaugurated a double expansion of Christian Spain, now unified under the rule of Ferdinand of Aragon and Isabella of Castile: toward the new world of America discovered by Columbus in the same year, and across the Straits of Gibraltar to North Africa. Muslim refugees from Spain crowded into the ports and cities of Morocco, Algeria, and Tunisia; and, resolved to continue the fight against the "infidels," they began to organize naval strikes at Spanish shipping. This was the beginning of "Barbary piracy." The campaign was probably launched by Kemal-Reis, who was sent by Sultan Bayezid II, in response to an appeal for help from the last Moorish sovereign of Granada, to ravage the Spanish coasts. Kemal, an able commander, became the terror of Christian navigators and was soon joined by his young nephew Piri, who was destined for a long career as a Turkish admiral. In 1517, when Sultan Selim was in Cairo after the final destruction of the Mamluk state, Piri presented to him a map of the world, which, according to his own account, he had compiled in 1513 from a number of medieval mappae mundi, Arabic maps of India, Portuguese charts, and a "map of Colon (Columbus)." In 1929 a portion of Piri's map, covering the Atlantic and its coasts, was found in the old imperial library in Istanbul: It shows the West Indies and the eastern coast of South America and is covered with manuscript notes and comments in Turkish, the longest of which gives a fairly accurate summary of Columbus's voyages. It must almost certainly be the first

Muslim map of America. As Piri mentions in his Bahriye, *a handbook of navigation he wrote in 1520-23, that he and his uncle captured seven Spanish vessels off Valencia in 1501, it is conjectured that a copy of the "Columbus map" may have been on board one of them. The original has never been found. As Piri submitted his map to Selim immediately after the conquest of Egypt, he may have hoped to interest the Sultan in the affairs of the Maghrib and persuade him to take the lead in a* jihad *against the Spaniards. Two years later, indeed, Selim appointed the famous corsair Khair ad-Din Barbarossa as Ottoman* beylerbey, *or governor, of North Africa, and Turkish domination was extended into the western Mediterranean. Extracts from the commentary on Piri's map follow.*

The author of this is the poor man Piri b. Haji Muhammad, who is known as the son of the brother of Kemal Reis, in the town of Gallipoli—may God have mercy on them both!—in the holy Muharram of the year 919 [=A.D. 1513].

This poor man had previously constructed a map which, in comparison with maps hitherto known, displayed many more and different details, and in which he had included even the newly published maps of the Indian and Chinese Oceans which at that time were totally unknown in the country of Rum [i.e., the Ottoman Empire], and he had presented it in Cairo to the Turkish Sultan Selim I, who graciously accepted it. . . . A map similar to this map has no one seen in this age.

[Against the Antilles is written:] These coasts are called the Antilia shores. They were discovered in the year 896 of the Arabic era. [An error, this would be equivalent to the year 1490-91, instead of 1492.] In the following manner it is reported: a Genoese infidel called Colon-bo was the first to find these territories. It is said that into the hand of this Colon-bo came a book which states that the Western Sea [the Atlantic] has an end, that on the side of the sunset are coasts and islands, and many different kinds of mines, and also a mountain of precious stones. In this book he finds it, he reads it right through, and explains these things to the eminent men of Genoa in detail and says: "Give me two ships, I will go forth and

"A Lost Map of Columbus" by P. Kahle. From *Geographical Review*, Oct. 23, 1933, pp. 621, 624-5, 638. Reprinted with permission of the American Geographical Society. A photograph of Piri's map, or rather of the half of it which survives, is reproduced at pp. 622-23 of the article.

seek these regions." They say: "O you simpleton, in the west is to be found the end and extremity of the world and its boundary; it is full of the vapour of darkness" so they say. The said Colon-bo sees that from the Genoese there is no help, makes inquiries, and goes to the Bey [King] of Spain, to whom he submits the story in detail. They also give him the same answer as the Genoese. But in the end Colon-bo becomes very insistent to them. Finally the Bey of Spain gives two ships, sees to their equipment, and says: "O Colon-bo, if it is as you say, then I will make you Capadan [captain, governor] over this territory." With these words he sent this Colon-bo to the Western Sea.

The late Ghazi Kemal [Piri's uncle] had a Spanish slave. This slave said: "Three times have I travelled with Colon-bo to this territory."

27 / THE ESTABLISHMENT OF OTTOMAN POWER IN NORTH AFRICA

Professor A. J. Toynbee, in his Study of History, *II, 444, remarks that had the Ottomans been able to make their power felt in the western Mediterranean thirty years earlier than they did, they might have saved Granada and stopped the Spaniards' discovering America. Their failure to do so was partly a consequence of the Jem affair and partly preoccupation with the Safavid threat from Persia. When they were at last free to act in the West, Spain had already gained several footholds in North Africa: Melilla in 1497, Oran in 1509, Algiers, Bougie, and Tripoli in 1510. The Spaniards were animated by an ardent crusading zeal; "Africa for King Ferdinand!" was their slogan at the time. The Barbary Muslims, reinforced by refugees from Granada, hit back to the best of their ability but were soon driven to seek Ottoman assistance. Two remarkable brothers from the Aegean island of Lesbos, or Mitylene, Aruj and Khair ad-Din, offered their services as independent corsairs and were granted bases on the coasts of what are now Algeria and Tunisia from which to attack Christian shipping. In 1516 King Ferdinand died, and the people of Algiers seized the chance to rebel and called in Aruj to bombard the Spanish-held fort of the Peñon, which commanded the town.*

Aruj developed political ambitions, and he and his brother established themselves almost as independent princes in Barbary. Aruj, however, was killed at Tlemcen in 1518; the Turkish newcomers made themselves unpopular with the native Arabs and Berbers, and Khair ad-Din, the surviving brother, deemed it prudent to place himself under the suzerainty of the Ottoman sultan. Selim confirmed him in his position, gave him military and financial aid, and the great corsair acted in future as Ottoman beylerbey, commander in chief or governor. In this more or less unplanned fashion, Ottoman power was extended to the western Mediterranean. "Barbarossa" drove the Spaniards from the Peñon in 1529 and captured Tunis in 1534, the Muslim position in North Africa being strengthened by these successes as well as by the conflict between the Emperor Charles V and Francis I of France. This situation actually produced in 1538 an Ottoman-French alliance, as a result of which Khair ad-Din helped the French take Nice from the imperialists. Charles V failed in his attempts to capture Tunis in 1535 and Algiers in 1541, but Spanish control of Sicily posed a constant threat to Muslim Barbary.

In the mid-seventeenth century the history of the Ottoman navy was written by Hajji Khalfa, perhaps the greatest of Turkish scholars. Here he describes how the Sultan's authority was acknowledged in Algiers in 1519.

At this time there was in the harbour opposite the castle of Jezaier [Algiers] a small fortress on an island about an arrow-shot from the city. The Spanish infidels had by some means obtained possession of this castle, and had thus in a manner shut in the inhabitants of the town. The unfortunate Algerines were therefore obliged to submit to them and pay tribute: till at last the oppression of the infidels became insupportable, and they wrote a letter of invitation to Oruj [Aruj] Reis. This letter Oruj received at Jajl and having perused it, made preparations for his departure. The castle of Jajl he gave in charge to his brother, and came to Algiers. There being here no regular governor, he entered the town and took up his abode in it. . . . The castle being in a dilapidated state, Oruj Reis was repairing the breaches when the enemy made a sudden assault, and erected their standard on the fortifications. Oruj Reis now led on his heroes against them, and a hot engagement ensued. By the favour of God they were again crowned

From *History of the Maritime Wars of the Turks* by Hajji Khalfa. English trans., Oriental Translation Fund, London, 1831, pp. 31-36.

with victory, and succeeded in taking the standard of the infidels, whom they pursued and killed while flying to their ships. Only one thousand of them escaped, who entering their ships, set sail and departed. After this Oruj Reis settled in Algiers, and the infidels were constantly harried and routed. He then sent information of his victory to [his brother] Khair ad-Din, to whom he offered the charge of the castle. . . .

[Oruj was shortly afterward killed at Tlemcen, and Khair ad-Din repelled a Spanish attack on Algiers.]

During these transactions, Khair ad-Din assembled the citizens of Algiers and addressed them in these words: "Hitherto I have given you every assistance, and I have fortified your castle by placing in it 400 pieces of cannon; now appoint whom you please as your governor, and I will proceed by sea to some other place." All of them simultaneously began to cry out and beseech him not to leave them. Khair ad-Din answered that the begs of Tunis and Tlemcen were opposed to him, but that if the *khotba* and the coinage were made in the name of the Ottoman Sultan, he would consent to remain with them. To this they agreed; and Khair ad-Din, having fitted out four vessels and loaded them with spoils, arms and various presents, and also forty valiant youths selected from among the prisoners, sent them as a present to Sultan Selim. The illustrious emperor graciously accepted them, and in return sent him a splendid sabre and dress of honour, with a *sanjak* [standard], which he gave in charge to one Haji Hussein, a servant of the Sublime Porte. But on their way to Algiers, eight Venetian galleys attacked them, and killed all the servants of Khair Beg. Haji Hussein with three others escaped, and landed at Motone [Modon, in Greece], whence he returned to the capital. On application to the Venetian governor, the ships were restored, and they once more set out for Algiers. On their arrival Khair ad-Din came out to meet them, and received with profound reverence the horse and sanjak, which the emperor had sent him. He then assembled his *divan* [council] and ordered the criers to proclaim the authority of the Sultan.

28 / ARAB-MUSLIM CONTROL OVER INDIA'S OVERSEAS TRADE IN THE FIFTEENTH CENTURY

The great turning point in relations between Islam and the West in the modern period was the Portuguese discovery of the Cape route to India in 1497-98, which brought the European Powers, for the first time in history, into the Indian Ocean. Chinese fleets had occasionally been seen there, especially in the early days of the Ming dynasty (1368-1644), but since about 1440 the Muslim states had enjoyed a virtual monopoly and the trade of India and the Far East was in their hands, as the following passage from the pen of a present-day Indian historian explains.

No account of India's overseas trade during this period will be complete without some reference to the nearly complete hold exercised over the same by the Arabs and Persians, as well as the foreign and semi-foreign Muslims living on Indian soil, until the practical monopoly was destroyed by the systematic naval attacks of the Portuguese. In the great city of Cambay, at the time of Ibn Battutah's visit [about A.D. 1346], foreign merchants formed the majority of the population, and they vied with one another in building fine houses and wonderful mosques which made Cambay one of the most beautiful cities visited by the traveller. In the neighbouring seaport of Gandhar a Muslim merchant was the owner of six ships, one of which, carrying an escort of fifty archers and fifty Abyssinian soldiers, was offered to Ibn Battutah for the transport of his mission sent out from the court of Delhi to China. Mention is made likewise of a Muslim shipowner of Calicut owning many ships with which he traded with China on the one side and Fars and Yemen on the other. The Shiah [Shi'a] community of Quilon was so rich that one of them could buy a ship with its whole cargo for loading the same with his own merchandise. By contrast the Hindu traders appear to have been almost wholly confined to the inland trade.

By the beginning of the sixteenth century, as we learn from the

"Economic Condition" in "The Delhi Sultanate" by U. N. Ghoshal from *The History and Culture of the Indian People*, vol. 6, pp. 651-54. Copyright © 1960 by Bharatiya Vidya Bhavan. Bombay. Reprinted with permission of the Bharatiya Vidya Bhavan.

detailed account of Barbosa, India's overseas trade with western Asia and eastern Africa was almost completely controlled by the foreign and semi-foreign Muslim merchants living outside and within her shores. We hear, it is true, of wealthy Hindu merchants of the Baniya caste belonging to the kingdom of Gujarat as well as of those living in the seaports of the Deccan and Malabar. But these appear to have been engaged mostly, if not wholly, in the distributing trade at the ports. The great Hindu merchants of Gujarat are expressly mentioned as trafficking with their own folk. More than half a century earlier, Ma Huan described the rich Chetty merchants of Cochin and Calicut as engaged in selling to the strangers arriving at these ports precious stones, pearls, aromatics and coral beads at standard rates. Altogether exceptional is the instance of Cannamore, where Hindu as well as Muslim merchants are described by Barbosa as sailing in their own ships as far as Ormuz. On the other hand, not only are Arabs and Persians mentioned as visiting Indian ports like Dabhol and Goa in many ships for trade, but the foreign Muslims of Gujarat are expressly stated to be trading in their own ships with the western lands. The foreigners in Calicut, consisting of Arabs and Persians as well as immigrants from Gujarat and the Deccan, made their great annual voyages to Aden and the Red Sea coast, the volume of their imports and exports being sufficiently impressive. The Cambay merchants, engaged in the immensely profitable trade with East Africa, and the merchants from other Indian ports trading similarly with Ormuz and Aden, must have belonged almost wholly to the class of foreign Muslim settlers. Indeed we are expressly told that foreign Muslim merchants lived in large numbers in Goa and other ports.

Let us next turn to India's coastal trade. According to Barbosa, the Mappillas (descendants of Arab colonists by their union with local women), living in Malabar, were owners of large ships, and they so completely controlled the trade and navigation of this land as to suggest to the observant traveller that but for the arrival of the Portuguese it would have come under Muslim rule. To this class doubtless belonged the enterprising Malabaris who mostly controlled, as we have seen, the trade along the western coast. Many Muslim ships, almost certainly belonging to the Mappillas, are described as visiting every year Pulicat, the great Indian market for

Burmese rubies at that time. Coromandel was included among the lands visited in their own ships by the foreign merchants belonging to the above mentioned "city of Bengala." . . .

While the predominance of the Muslim traders in lands under rulers of their own faith requires little or no explanation, their command of the trade in the independent Hindu kingdoms is proved by the contemporary evidence to have been actively promoted and fostered by the policy of the kings—a policy which is in line with age-old indigenous tradition. From the vivid narrative of Ibn Battutah, we learn that the Hindu ruler of Malabar provided wooden houses with walls at every half mile, with special arrangements for the comfort of Muslim travellers, along the great coastal road of two months' journey from Sandapur (near Goa) to Quilon. Because of the death penalty inflicted by these rulers without any discrimination for rank, even for the slightest theft (of which concrete and harrowing instances are given by the traveller), no road, according to his very experienced judgment, was safer than this. The Hindu ruler of Calicut extended this security to the goods of shipwrecked merchants, so that the town became, in the words of Ibn Battutah, very flourishing and drew a great influx of foreigners. The Hindu ruler of Quilon was especially noted for his high regard for Muslims who were much honoured in his kingdom. The colonies of Muslims in every city of Malabar lived under the jurisdiction of their own *qazis* [cadis, judges] and worshipped freely in their big congregational mosques.

In the early part of the sixteenth century, according to the vivid account of Barbosa, the Muslims enjoyed the same patronage from the Hindu rulers of the south. We have seen how the Mappillas of Malabar had acquired by that time such complete control over the trade and navigation of the land as to bring it, according to the considered judgment of the writer, to the brink of subjection to Muslim rule. Their numbers were being constantly swelled by voluntary conversion of the Hindu men and women and their own union with Hindu concubines of low caste. The foreign merchants of Calicut, who had their own governors for ruling and punishing them without interference from the king, were so numerous and powerful as completely to dominate the city until they were forced to abandon it under pressure of the Portuguese. It was their custom on their return voyages from the Red Sea ports every year to bring with them fresh foreign merchants, each of whom on his arrival was assigned by the king a Nayan bodyguard, a Chetty accountant, and a broker for help in local purchases. In the preceding century Ma Huan found that all the affairs of the Calicut kingdom were conducted by two high Muslim officers who controlled the sale of all the merchandise brought into the city in Chinese junks. In the neighbouring territory of Kayal at the time of Barbosa's visit, the Hindu ruler had farmed out for long the rich monopoly of the local pearl fisheries to a Muslim, who was so rich and powerful as to be honoured equally with the king. In Vijayanagar the complete freedom of travel and worship granted by the king to everybody "without enquiry whether he was Christian, Jew, Moor or heathen," as well as the great equity and justice shown to all by the ruler and his subjects, drew an enormous number of merchants to the city. Great Muslim as well as Hindu merchants lived at Pulicat, the frontier station of the Vijayanagar kingdom, which was likewise visited by Muslim ships in large numbers for trade.

29 / VASCO DA GAMA ARRIVES AT CALICUT, 1498

The Portuguese, under Bartholomew Diaz, rounded the Cape of Good Hope in 1488. Nine years later an expedition commanded by Vasco da Gama sailed from Lisbon on the first historic voyage round Africa to India. The last stage of this voyage, from Malindi in East Africa to Calicut in south India, is described by a near contemporary Portuguese historian, Fernão Lopes de Castanheda, whose History of the Discovery and Conquest of India *was published in 1552.*

Having thus procured a pilot, and provided all things necessary for the voyage, da Gama departed from Malindi for Calicut on Friday, April 26, 1498, and immediately made sail directly across the gulf which separates Africa from India. This gulf runs a long way up into the land northwards; but our course for Calicut lay to the east. In following this voyage, our men saw the north star the next Sunday, which they had not seen for a long while. They

From *History of the Discovery and Conquest of India* by Fernão Lopes de Castanheda, trans. by Nicholas Lichefield in *General History and Collection of Voyages and Travels* edited by Robert Kerr, Edinburgh, 1824, II, 343-59.

gave thanks to God, that whereas it had been represented to them that in this season, which was the winter of the Indies, there were always great storms in this gulf, they now experienced fair weather. On Friday May 18, twenty-three days after leaving Malindi, during all which time they had seen no land, they came in sight of India, the land seeming very high. Canaca, the pilot, tried the lead and found 45 fathoms, upon which he altered his course to the southeast, having fallen in with the land too far to the north. Upon the Saturday, he again drew near the land, but did not certainly know it, as the view was obscured by rain, which always falls in India at this season, being their winter. On Sunday May 20, the pilot got view of certain high hills which are directly behind the city of Calicut, and came so near the land that he was quite sure of the place; and on which he came up with great joy to the general [da Gama], demanding his reward, as this was the place at which he and his company were so desirous to arrive. The general was greatly rejoiced at the news, and immediately satisfied the pilot, after which he summoned all the company to prayers, saying the *salve,* and giving hearty thanks to God, who had safely conducted them to the long wished for place of his destination. When prayer was over, there was great festivity and joy in the ships, which came that same evening to anchor two leagues from Calicut. Immediately upon anchoring, some of the natives came off to the ships in four boats, inquiring whence our ships came, as they had never before seen any resembling their construction upon that coast. These natives were of a brown colour, and entirely naked, excepting very small aprons. Some of them came on board, and the Gujarati pilot informed the general that they were poor fishermen; yet the general received them courteously, and ordered his people to purchase the fish which they had brought for sale. On conversing with them, he understood that the town whence they came, which was in sight, was not Calicut, which lay farther off, and to which they offered to conduct our fleet. Whereupon the general requested them to do this; and departing from this first anchorage, the fleet was conducted by these fishermen to Calicut.

Calicut is a city on the coast of Malabar. . . . In ancient times this country of Malabar was entirely ruled by one king. In the reign of the last king of this race, who died 600 years ago [i.e., about

A.D. 950], the Moors [Arab Muslims] of Mecca discovered India, and came to the province of Malabar, then inhabited by idolaters, and governed by an idolatrous king. After the coming of the Moors into Malabar, they insinuated themselves so much into the confidence of the before-mentioned king, that he became a convert to their law, renouncing the religion of his country, and embracing Muhammadanism with such zeal that he resolved to go and end his days in the temple of Mecca [the Ka'ba]. Because this king embarked from this place on his pilgrimage to Mecca, the Moors have ever since held Calicut in so high devotion that they and all their posterity would never take their lading from any other port. . . .

As the Moors are merchants of most extensive dealings, they have rendered Calicut, as the centre of their trade, the richest mart of all India; in which is to be found all the spices, drugs, nutmegs, and other things that can be desired, all kinds of precious stones, pearls and seed-pearls, musk, sanders [sandalwood], fine dishes of earthenware, lacquer, gilded coffers, and all the fine things of China, gold, amber, wax, ivory, fine and coarse cotton goods, both white and dyed of many colours, much raw and twisted silk, stuffs of silk and gold, cloth of gold, cloth of tissue, grain, scarlets, silk carpets, copper, quicksilver, vermilion, alum, coral, rosewater and all kinds of conserves. . . . Calicut is surrounded by many gardens and orchards, producing all the herbs and fruits of this country in great abundance, having also many palms and other sorts of trees, and abounds in excellent water. The city is large, but the dwellings consist only of straw huts; their idol temples and chapels and the king's palace excepted, which are built of stone and lime and covered with tiles. At this time Calicut was inhabited by idolaters of many sects, and by many Moorish merchants, some of whom were so rich as to be owners of fifty ships. . . . The prince in the language of the country was styled the Zamorin, which signifies Emperor; . . . he was a Brahmin, as his predecessors had been, the Brahmins being priests among the Malabars. . . .

Having come to anchor on the outside of the bar or reef of Calicut, the general sent one of the Portuguese on shore, instructing him to see what kind of place it was, and to make trial of what kind of a reception might be looked for, seeing we were Christians. When this man landed, he was immediately surrounded by great numbers of the natives, staring at him as a stranger. These people asked of the fishermen what man this was whom they had brought on shore? to which they answered that they supposed him to be a Moor, and that he belonged to the three ships which were riding without the bar. But the people of Calicut wondered much to see a person who was clothed so very differently from the Moors who came from the Red Sea. Some of these people who had knowledge of Arabic spoke to this man, but he could not understand or answer them, at which they were much astonished. Yet believing him to be a Moor, they conducted him to a house where two Moors dwelt who came originally from Tunis and had established themselves in Calicut. On his appearance, one of the Moors, who was called Bontaybo and who could speak Spanish, immediately recognized him for a Portuguese, having often seen people of our nation at Tunis. As soon as he saw the Portuguese, he exclaimed in Spanish, "Devil take you, what brought you here?" He further inquired which way he had traveled so as to arrive at Calicut? To this the man answered, telling how many ships our general had brought with him, at which the Moor was much amazed, wondering how they could possibly come by sea from Portugal to India. He then asked what they sought at so great a distance from home? And was answered that they came in search of Christians and spices. After some further conversation, the Moor gave him good entertainment, commanding certain cakes of wheat flour and honey to be set before him; and then said he would accompany him to the ships to wait upon the general.

Bontaybo accordingly came on board to our general, whom he immediately addressed in Spanish, saying: "Good luck, good luck! many rubies, many emeralds. You should give God thanks for bringing you where there is abundance of all sorts of spices and precious stones." On hearing this, the general and all the people were greatly astonished, not expecting to meet anyone so far from home who understood their language. . . . The general requested information from Bontaybo as to the character of the king or Zamorin of Calicut and whether in his opinion he would willingly receive him as ambassador from the King of Portugal. Bontaybo represented the Zamorin as a prince of good and honourable disposition who, he was convinced, would gladly receive the general as ambassador

from a foreign king, more especially if the object of his voyage were
to establish a trade with Calicut. . . . The general called a council
of the other captains and principal officers of his fleet, to whom
he intimated his intention of going to visit the king of Calicut on
purpose to settle a treaty of trade and amity. Paulo da Gama, his
brother, strongly objected to his venturing on shore; alleging there
were many Moors among the people who were to be feared as his
mortal enemies; since the people at Mozambique and Mombasa,
where they had only passed by their ports, endeavoured to destroy
them all, they were much more to be feared at Calicut, where we
had come on purpose to enter into competition with them in trade,
by which their profits would be diminished.

30 / ARAB REACTION TO THE PORTUGUESE INTRUSION

*The Arab, Egyptian, and Indian Muslims, who had so long con-
trolled the commerce of the Indian Ocean, were taken completely
by surprise by the sudden apppearance of the "Franks" of the Christian West in an area where they had never been seen before. Their
bewilderment and anger is vividly revealed in these passages from a
contemporary Arab chronicle composed in the Hadramawt, the in-
cense land of south Arabia: In them we may trace the progress of
the Portuguese intrusion, the efforts of the Egyptian Mamluks to
check it, the naval battle off Diu in 1509, and the successful defense of Aden against the Europeans in 1513. The term "Frank"
used here is, so to speak, the counterpart of "Moor": It was employed by the Arabs to designate all West Europeans, whether Ital-
ians, Spaniards, Portuguese, French, Dutch, or English.*

Year 904 [A.D. 1498-99]
In this year the infidel Franks appeared off Mogadishu and Sabaj
[unknown place] in India. Their course ran under the wind, and
he [the Frank] made for Kilwa, where he built a fort.

Year 906 [A.D. 1500-01]
Then after him [Mamluk Sultan Ka'itbai] his slave Kansuh al-
Ghuri came to power. He despatched a mighty fleet to fight the
Frank, its commander being Husain Kurdi. Entering India, he

From the Hadrami chronicles, cited in *The Portuguese off the South Arabian
Coasts* by R. B. Serjeant. Copyright © 1963 by the Clarendon Press, Oxford.
Reprinted with permission of the publisher.

stopped at Diu, the monarch of which was Sultan Mahmud. . . . This was at the first appearance of the Franks (may God curse them!) in the [Indian] Ocean, plundering Muslim shipping.

Year 908 [A.D. 1502-03]

In this year the vessels of the Franks appeared at sea en route for India, Hurmuz [Ormuz] and those parts. They took about seven vessels, killing those on board and making some prisoners. This was their first action (may God curse them!).

Year 912 [A.D. 1506-07]

In this year the power of the Franks became strengthened, and great damage was caused by them in certain parts of India.

Year 913 [A.D. 1507-08]

In this year the Franks (may God abandon them!) gained control over the island of Socotra and the island of Hurmuz.

In this year there also arrived from Jeddah [Jidda] Husain Kurdi, in command of three grabs [large coasting vessels] and three galliots [small swift galleys], making towards India. He took the course towards Diu with his sailing-ships in order to engage the Franks who had appeared in the [Indian] Ocean and cut the Muslims' trade-routes.

Year 914 [A.D. 1508-09]

In this year the Franks took Dabul [Debal, or Daybul], looting and burning it. In this year also the Franks made an expedition against Gujarat and attacked Diu. The Amir Husain, who was at that time in Diu fighting the Holy War, went forth to meet him and they fought an engagement at sea beyond the port. Many on the Frankish side were slain, but eventually the Franks prevailed over the Muslims, and there befell a great slaughter among the Amir Husain's soldiers, about 600 men, while the survivors fled to Diu.

Year 919 [A.D. 1513-14]

The Franks (may God abandon them!) arrived before the port of Aden. They advanced on the town, scaling the walls there with ladders. Those who took part in the manoeuvre numbered about 2000, along with ample equipment. The people fled before them and all hearts were filled with trepidation. Then God granted the Muslims victory, and they routed them, cutting them down with frightful slaughter. A number of Muslims won martyrdom for the faith . . . [and] of the Franks about 200 were slain.

31 / THE FIRST EUROPEAN ENTERS MECCA AND MEDINA, 1503

While the Portuguese were creating havoc in the Indian Ocean and successfully challenging Islam on the high seas, an intrepid Italian traveler set out on a lone tour of southern Asia, in the course of which he became the first European to penetrate the Holy Cities of Arabia, entry to which has always been barred to "infidels." This was Ludovico di Varthema, of whose life, apart from what we learn from his Travels, little is known. Varthema is a place near Bologna. Ludovico left Italy at the end of 1502 and landed in Egypt, whence he went to Syria and at Damascus joined the Mecca pilgrimage in the guise of a Muslim. After accomplishing this daring venture without mishap, he explored the Yemen, took ship at Aden for Persia and India, visited Ceylon, crossed the Bay of Bengal to Malaya, and got as far east as the Moluccas, returning to Europe via East Africa and the Cape. He reached Lisbon in 1508 and thence crossed to Italy, publishing his Itinerario (Travels) at Rome in 1510. The book instantly became popular and was translated into Latin and the leading languages of Europe. Ludovico's later history is unknown; we have no record of the time or place of his death. The accuracy of his observations is remarkable, and the details he gives of Mecca and Medina have been completely confirmed by later European travelers such as Burckhardt and Burton, who ran the same risks as he did.

Ludovico noted the economic difficulties into which the Muslims were falling because the Indian trade was being seriously interrupted by the Portuguese, who were in fact planning to take Aden and move up the Red Sea to seize the Holy Cities themselves, thereby striking what they thought would be a mortal blow at the heart of Islam. Their repulse from the walls of Aden in 1513 frustrated this design.

The next day we resumed our journey, and in two days' time arrived at a city which is called Medinathalnabi [Medina al-Nabi—

From *The Travels of Ludovico di Varthema, 1503-1508.* The Hakluyt Society, London, 1863, pp. 25-31, 38-41, 49-51.

"City of the Prophet"]. Near that city at a distance of four miles we found a well, by which the caravan halted for a day, and at this well each person washed himself, and put on clean linen to go into the said city, which contains about 300 hearths, and is surrounded by walls made of earth. The houses within are constructed of stone walls. The country around the said city lies under the curse of God, for the land is barren, with the exception that about two stones' cast, outside the city, there are about fifty or sixty feet of palmtrees in a garden, at the end of which there is a certain conduit of water, which descends at least twenty-four steps, of which water the caravan takes possession when it arrives there. Now some who say that the body of Mahomet is suspended in the air at Mecca must be reproved; I say that it is not true. I have seen his sepulchre in this city, Medinathalnabi, in which we remained three days, and wished to see everything. The first day we went into the city, at the entrance by the door of their mosque, and each of us, small or great, was obliged to be accompanied by some person, who took us by the hand, and led us to where Mahomet was buried. The mosque is made square in this manner: being about 100 paces long, and 80 wide, and it has around it two doors or three sides, and the roof made arched, and there are more than 400 columns made of burnt stone, all whitened, and there are about 3000 lighted lamps burning on one side of the arches. On the right hand, at the head of the mosque, there is a square tower, about five paces on every side, which tower has a cloth of silk around it. At the distance of two paces from the said tower there is a very beautiful grating of metal, where persons stand to see the said tower, and at one side on the left there is a little door which leads you to the said tower, and in the said tower there is another little door, and by one of the doors there are about twenty books, and on the other side there are about twenty-five books, which are those of Mahomet and his companions, which books declare his life and the command-ments of his sect. Within the said door there is a sepulchre, that is, a pit underground, wherein was placed Mahomet, also Haly [Ali], and Babacher [Abu Bakr], and Othman, and Aumar [Omar], and Fatone [Fatima]. . . . And you must know (I tell it you for a truth) there is no coffin of iron or steel, nor lodestone, nor any mountain within four miles. . . .

[After thus refuting from his own personal observation the foolish tale long current in Europe that Muhammad's coffin was suspended in midair by the action of powerful magnets or lodestones, Ludovico goes on to describe the Ka'ba, or Holy House, of Mecca.]

In the midst of the same city [Mecca] there is a very beautiful temple, similar to the Colosseum of Rome, but not made of such large stones, but of burnt bricks, and it is round in the same manner; it has ninety or a hundred doors around it, and is arched. On entering the said temple, you descend ten or twelve steps of marble . . . and when you have descended the said steps you find the said temple all around, and everything, that is, the walls, covered with gold. . . . Within the said temple, and uncovered, and in the centre, there is a tower [the Ka'ba], the size of which is about five or six paces on every side, around which tower there is a cloth of black silk [the *kiswah*, renewed annually, and now made of silk and cotton]. And there is a door all of silver, of the height of a man, by which you enter the said tower. . . . On the 24th of May [1503] all the people began before day to go seven times round the said tower, always touching and kissing each corner [more exactly, kissing the sacred Black Stone, let into the eastern corner of the Ka'ba, which Ludovico does not mention]. In the centre of the said tower there is a very beautiful well, which is seventy fathoms deep, and the water is brackish. At this well there stand six or eight men appointed to draw water for the people. And when the said people have gone seven times around the first tower, they go to this well, and place themselves with their backs towards the brink of this well, saying, "In the name of God, pardon my sins." And those who draw the water throw three bucketsful over each person, from the crown of their heads to their feet, and all bathe, even though their dress be of silk. And they say in this wise, that all their sins remain there [i.e., in the well] after this washing. . . .

Having gone to make some purchases for my captain [of the caravan], I was recognized by a Moor, who looked me in the face and said, "Where are you from?" I answered, "I am a Moor." He replied, "You are not telling the truth." I said to him, "By the head of Mahomet, I am a Moor." He answered, "Come to my house," and I went with him. When I had arrived at his house, he spoke to me in Italian, and told me where I came from, and that he knew I was not a Moor, and he told me he had been in Genoa and Venice, and gave me proofs of it. When I heard this, I told him that I was a Roman, and had become a Mameluke at Cairo. When he heard this he was much pleased, and treated me with very great honour, and as it was my intention to proceed further, I began to say to him, if this was the city of Mecca which was so renowned through all the world, where were the jewels and spices, and where were the various kinds of merchandise which it was reported were brought there. I asked him this only that he might tell me why they had not arrived as usual, and in order not to ask him if the King of Portugal was the cause, he being Lord of the Mare Oceano [the Atlantic] and the Persian and Arabian Gulfs. Then he began to tell me by degrees why the said articles had not come as they were accustomed to do. And when he told me that the King of Portugal was the cause, I pretended to be much grieved, and spoke great ill of the said king, merely that he might not think that I was pleased that the Christians should make such a journey.

32 / THE OTTOMAN CHALLENGE TO THE PORTUGUESE

The Mamluks were the first to challenge the Portuguese intruders, mainly because the economic well-being of their kingdom was being imperiled, but the destruction of their fleet off Diu in 1509 and the growing menace of the Ottomans rendered them unable to give much succor to the Arab-Indian Muslims. When the Ottomans conquered Egypt and Syria in 1516-17, they had to take over the defense of Islam in this region, and the Muslim sultanates in India now looked to Constantinople for help. Under Sulaiman the Magnificent (1520-66) a series of naval expeditions was dispatched to the East in an effort to break the Portuguese stranglehold on Muslim commerce in the Indian Ocean. Hajji Khalfa here describes the fate of the one of 1538 and its unsuccessful attempt to capture Diu, which the Portuguese had made their principal strongpoint on the Indian coast.

Spain had just completed the conquest of the New World, and so early as the year 900 [A.D. 1494-95—a wrong date] the Portuguese,

From *History of the Maritime Wars of the Turks* by Hajji Khalfa. English Trans., Oriental Translation Fund, London, 1831, pp. 65-66.

emboldened by her success, proceeded from the Western to the
Eastern Ocean, and passing along the Mountains of the Moon
(where the blessed Nile has its source) and the coasts of Abyssinia
and Zanguebar [Zanzibar], penetrated into India, and took possession of the fortresses of Sind. The kings of that country being too
weak to resist them, the king of Guznat [Gujarat] applied for assistance to Sultan Sulaiman Khan. This zealous monarch, with the
view of driving the oppressive infidels from the coasts of Yemen
and India, equipped a fleet of thirty galleys in the road of Suez,
and gave the command of them to Khadem Sulaiman Pasha, chief
of the emirs of Egypt, who left the port of Suez about the end of
Moharrem 945 [A.D. 1538], and arrived on the seventh of Rabi al-avul
[the third month of the Muslim year] at the city of Aden, on the
coast of the Yemen, the fortresses of which he took possession of.
He then proceeded towards Div [Diu], an Indian port in possession
of the Portuguese, which was the principal object of his efforts.
The winds being favourable, he arrived at the citadels of Goa and
Kari, situated in the neighbourhood of Div, and also in possession
of the Portuguese, where he landed his men and artillery, and took
both these fortresses, one thousand infidels falling by the sword.
He next laid siege to Div, the citadel of which was defended on
three sides by the sea, and on the land side by very strong fortifications, on which account he deemed it advisable to land 20,000 men
and a considerable quantity of ammunition. The siege had now
lasted a month, and the king of Guznat had in vain expected the
ammunition and provisions he had demanded from Prince Mahmud.
This prince, frightened at the murder of Amar, the emir of Aden
[who had been hanged by Sulaiman on a charge of anti-Turkish
activity], would neither come himself nor send succours. The besieged infidels then, as a last resource, persuaded Mahmud that the
murder was committed by Sulaiman Pasha, and that any good the
latter might do to him would be dictated by treachery. This refusal,
together with his open opposition to them in other matters, and
the peace he had made with the infidels, obliged the Muslims to
raise the siege of the citadel.

33 / THE PORTUGUESE IN ABYSSINIA

The struggle between the Ottomans and the Portuguese had impor-
tant repercussions in Abyssinia, an ancient, large, and unwieldy
Christian kingdom hemmed in by Muslim territory. The Negus, its
king who claimed descent from Solomon, had little effective con-
trol outside the core of his kingdom; the people were barbarous,
the government primitive, and the remote provinces virtually inde-
pendent under feudal tribal chiefs. Along the Red Sea coast strong
Muslim principalities grew up in the late fifteenth century, and
the Abyssinians, alarmed at their isolation, began to seek contact
with the Portuguese as early as 1487. The Portuguese, surprised to
learn of this Christian state in the heart of Africa, identified it with
the realm of Prester John, which had hitherto been sought in Asia.
However, it was not until 1520 that a formal Portuguese mission
was sent to the Negus; it stayed six years in the country, but effected
little, as the reigning monarch, Lebna Dengel (1508-40), had in-
flicted some heavy defeats on the Muslims and was less ready to
accept foreign aid. Scarcely had it gone in 1526 when a frightful
storm burst over the country. A brilliant Somali warrior, Ahmad
b. Ibrahim, whom the Abyssinians called Gran ("the Left-Handed"),
built up a powerful fighting force, imbued his tribesmen with ardor
for the jihad, or holy war, against the Christian infidels, and in-
vaded the Negus's territories in 1527. In a few years his armies had
spread all over the south and center of Abyssinia, killing, burning
and plundering; the Muslim tribes usually welcomed the invaders,
and many Christian tribes apostatized to Islam. Threatened with
the total destruction of his kingdom, Lebna Dengel sent in 1535 a
desperate appeal to Portugal, but such was the slowness of com-
munications that not until 1541 did a Portuguese force of four hun-
dred matchlockmen arrive by sea. By then the Negus was dead, and
his son Claudius (1540-59) was striving as best he could to halt the
onrush of the Somalis. The coming of the Portuguese, though few
in number, raised the spirits of the hard-pressed Abyssinians; Ahmad,
for his part, got some cannon and musketeers from the Turks, but
gradually the tide turned against him, his nomadic warriors got out
of hand, and the Christian allies inflicted a decisive defeat on him
near Lake Tana in 1542. The left-handed conqueror was killed, his
kingdom collapsed, and Abyssinia was saved from Muslim conquest.
King Claudius's grateful letter to John III of Portugal, quoted
below, gives the Abyssinian version of these events. The Ottomans

might have intervened more effectively on the Muslim side but for their defeat off Diu in 1538. Even in the Red Sea their control was not complete, for a Portuguese squadron sailed up as far as Suez in 1541. As it was, Christianity in Abyssinia was saved; Muslim expansion in East Africa was halted, and the Portuguese were enabled to retain their grip on the commerce of the Indian Ocean, a grip ultimately broken, not by the Muslims, but by their fellow Europeans, the Dutch.

In 1527 the Imam Ahmad, surnamed Gran, or the left-handed, began his incursions into the country. The coquettings between the Portuguese and the Abyssinians had not escaped the vigilance of the Muhamadans, whose attention had previously been arrested by the early proceedings of the Europeans in India. After the defeat of the Egyptian fleet off Diu, by Almeida in 1509, the survivors escaped to Jidda to form the nucleus of a new armada. The defeat of the Sultan of Egypt by the Ottoman Turk in 1516 caused a temporary break in the continuity of Musalman policy; but the matter was never lost sight of. The actions of the Portuguese in the Red Sea meanwhile had been irritating to their opponents, without at the same time striking any definite blow at their power. Both Albuquerque in 1513 and Lopo Soares in 1517 spent the summer months there, and lost a very large proportion of their men through the climate and unsuitable food. They retired thoroughly disorganized, and so alarmed were the Portuguese at the results of these expeditions that no fleet, until that of D. Estevao da Gama, ever again attempted to spend any part of the year after March beyond the straits of Babelmandeb [Bab al-Mandab—"Gate of Tears"]. Albuquerque was defeated in his attempt to capture Aden; Lopo Soares was cajoled into not taking possession of it when it lay helpless at his mercy, and the Portuguese never had another opportunity to occupy it. They were thus reduced to a series of raids, burning coast towns and leaving ruined cities behind them to mark their track: proceedings which if they singed the Muhamadans' beard, certainly never weakened his power of offence.

The expedition which Sulaiman Pasha commanded in 1538 was

From *The Portuguese Expedition to Abyssinia, 1541-43*, ed. and trans. by R. S. Whiteway. The Hakluyt Society, London, 1902, Introduction, pp. xxxi-xxxiii. Reprinted with permission of the Hakluyt Society.

a complete failure, as far as regards the attack on Diu, but it secured to the Turks command of the Red Sea. On his return journey he left garrisons in all the important towns. It is true that in 1541 D. Estevao da Gama took his lighter vessels as far as Suez, but his return thence, when he found the strength of the Turkish force, was very like a flight; and the audacity of his enterprise thoroughly aroused the Turks, whose galleys from that date patrolled the sea, and rendered communication between Abyssinia and India an enterprise of danger. Firearms had been introduced into Arabia in 1515, and Muhamadan merchants, aided by the policy of the Turks, brought these weapons to Zeila [the Somali port, later held by Ahmad Gran]; as they had not at the time reached Abyssinia the relative power of Muhamadans and Christians was entirely changed, and the genius of the Imam Ahmad enabled him to take full advantage of the improved armament of his co-religionists. The Somali armies were accompanied by regular bodies of matchlockmen, who were usually Turks from Zebid, on the Arabian coast of the Red Sea. An olive tree standing in the Abyssinian centre was cut in two by the first cannon shot fired in one of the early battles; and then, as the Muhamadan chronicler puts it, "the Christians tumbled one on the other" and the Imam's army by an immediate charge won the victory. By 1533 the Christians had got one or two cannon, which were worked by renegade "Arabs," who from their names may have been a Turk and a Persian; the artillery opposed to them was managed, it is said, by Indians.

34 / THE KING OF ABYSSINIA DESCRIBES HOW THE PORTUGUESE HELPED HIM EXPEL THE MUSLIM INVADERS

In the name of the Holy Trinity, our Eternal Life, in which we believe, and which is our salvation. This letter is sent from the presence of the King of Ethiopia, Asnaf Sagad [Claudius], son of King Wanag Sagad, second son of King Naod, son of King Bdemaryan, son of King Zra Yakut, of the race of David and Solomon, Kings of Israel, greeting to the King of Portugal, Dom Joao [John],

From *The Portuguese Expedition to Abyssinia, 1541-43,* ed. and trans. by R. S. Whiteway. The Hakluyt Society, London, 1902, pp. 115-18. Reprinted with permission of the Hakluyt Society.

son of King Emmanuel. God make you a great Lord in the land, and place in your hand the sea, the islands and the continent. May he make you a greater lord in the heavens for all eternity, as he does to his friends and holy men. Through your prayers God worked us great good; with the help of your men we have conquered the Moors, and have always been victorious over them. The Captain Don Christovao landed from the sea and entered my country with 400 Franks, and many bombards and matchlocks and other arms. Numerous Moors collected against him. Our men were few, so that the day was not ours. I did not arrive in time to join the Captain, for I was far away in another country called Seoa [Shoa]. While Don Christovao was in Tigre, he sent me a messenger to ask me to come quickly, as it was necessary that we should both meet. The messenger reached me, he was called Ayres Dias, a servant of the Captain, called by the people of this country Marcos. When I heard the message, I began to march in haste, that we might join. On the way I heard that Ahmad had killed Don Christovao and many Franks, and captured all the bombards, munitions and weapons they had; and that the Franks who escaped were scattered over the country. At this news I was so sorrowful that I wept with sadness and passion. Ahmad with his own men alone could not defeat them. Besides his own men, he got over 600 Turks, with whose assistance as they were many, he obtained the victory. I marched at once to the country of Tigre, and collected the Franks who were scattered over the district: they were one hundred and thirty. Some others had gone to Bdebarrua to seek shipping to return to their country. I made Ayres Dias, whom the people of this country call Marcos, Captain of the hundred and thirty Portuguese in place of Don Christovao, and all the Franks were satisfied. After this we fought thrice with the Moors, and God gave us the victory. Once they came against us with 210 Turks, and with the bombards and pikes of the Franks, which were captured when Don Christovao was killed. Another time they came against us with eighty Turks, who were all killed, and also Ahmad was killed. In the end the Moors were so destroyed that very few of them remained, and nearly all the Turks were killed; and all their bombards and arms came into our power, and the power of the Franks of Portugal. All this benefit and these riches and all this good fortune came to us from our Brother and our Friend, our Blood and our Life, Jesus Christ. Don Christovao could not destroy the Moors; the fortunate Ayres Dias, his servant, with one hundred and thirty Franks defeated and destroyed them entirely, though Don Christovao had fought valiantly against the Moors. May God pardon his soul and place him among the martyrs. Amen. The Franks who are here live with me at their pleasure; they have much property and riches, which I have given them where they desire it. . . . Believe all this. Written in the year of Christ's birth 1542, according to the count of Ethiopia and Egypt, and according to the count of the Franks 1550; on the sixth day of the month of Christmas.

35 / THE OTTOMAN ECONOMY AND THE SHIFTING OF THE TRADE ROUTES

The economic and commercial consequences of the Ottoman conquest of the Near East have been much debated. The old theory was that the Turks "closed the trade routes" to the Christian Powers, who were thus driven to seek alternative means of reaching the East despite the fact that the Cape route was discovered in 1497-98 and the Turks did not occupy Syria and Egypt till 1516-17. Professor Lybyer, in a famous article published in 1915, made it clear that the Turks were only too anxious to keep open the old channels of trade, which were a source of great profit to them, and that the Portuguese entry into the Indian Ocean, which was unconnected with the policy or actions of the Turks, was a severe blow to the well-being of their Empire.

There is evidence to indicate that no one of the shorter routes, had there been no Turks nor any other nation on their lines to take toll of their wares, could have competed for the trade of southern Asia with western Europe against the Cape route. The land transit alone by the Persian Gulf route seems to have cost more than the sea freight from India to Europe. A calculation made about 1800 shows that a shipment from India to France by way of the Red Sea would probably make a profit of 4%, whereas the same consignment, if sent round the Cape, would earn from 36% to 48%: if a Christian power were in possession of the Red Sea and Egypt,

From "The Ottoman Turks and the Routes of Oriental Trade" by A. H. Lybyer. From *English Historical Review*, 1915, XXX, pp. 587-88.

the gain by that route would not be more than 10%. The Red Sea is so straight and narrow, and so strewn with rocks and shallows, that sailing-vessels have to wait for favourable winds and waste much time. The Indiamen were not well adapted to this sea, so that transhipment was customary at Aden, Moche or Jedda. There was always a transit by land, of some ninety miles at the shortest (from Suez to Cairo), then a passage by small vessel on the Nile, and another transhipment at Alexandria. On the other hand, the time necessary for a voyage between India and Europe averaged not much less by the Cape route than by the Red Sea. Until the invention of the steamship, which could run straight through the Red Sea without reference to the winds, and the excavation of the Suez Canal, which eliminated the land transit, the Cape route seems to have been cheaper than all others for long-distance wares.

It appears that the relation of the Turks to the change of trade routes has been misconceived. They were not active agents in deliberately obstructing the routes. They did not by their notorious indifference and conservatism greatly, if at all, on the whole increase the difficulties of the oriental traffic. Nor did they make the discovery of new routes imperative. On the contrary, they lost by the discovery of a new and superior route. Had there been no way round Africa, the whole story of the Levant since 1500 might have been very different. In the first place, the Mameluke Sultans might have found in their uninterrupted traffic sufficient financial support to enable them to resist successfully the attack of the Turks in 1516. But if the Turks had conquered Egypt while the full stream of oriental trade ran through it, they must either have been deprived far sooner than was actually the case of the control of these routes, or they would have had to accommodate themselves to the great and increasing trade through their dominions. In the latter case they might have been forced into adopting modern ways, and adding to their wonderful capacity for territorial unification a parallel scheme of organizing their trade. The decay of the lands of the Levant (neglecting the hypothesis of climatic change) might have been arrested and reversed. But there was a Cape route, and for three centuries and a half it took the bulk of the oriental trade. Selim I and Sulaiman, the greatest of the Ottoman conquerors, were powerless in their efforts to bring back the lucrative flow of Eastern wares.

The shifting of the trade routes was done, not by the Turks, but in their despite and to their disadvantage. The desolation of Egypt and Syria, the decline of the Italian cities, perhaps the very decay of the Ottoman Empire itself, are due, not to them, but to the great discoveries, in which, positively or negatively, they had no discernible part.

36 / THE REVOLUTION IN WORLD COMMUNICATIONS AROUND 1500

The following extract from Professor A. J. Toynbee reminds us how the great land empires of Islam—of the Ottomans and the Moguls, above all—were confronted in the sixteenth century by a Western Europe which had found a way of turning the Muslim flank by a sea approach. The result was a big and permanent shift in the world's principal trade routes. The oceans replaced the steppes as the main highway of commerce.

For human purposes, the Steppe was an inland sea which, in virtue of happening to be dry, was of higher conductivity for human intercourse than the salt-water sea ever was before the close of the fifteenth century of the Christian era. This waterless sea had its dry-shod ships with quayless ports. The steppe-galleons were camels, the steppe-galleys horses, and the steppe-ports "caravan cities"—ports of call on oasis-islands and termini on the coasts where the sand-waves of the "Desert" broke upon the "Sown": Petra and Palmyra, Damascus and Ur, Tamerlane's Samarkand and the Chinese emporia at the gates of the Great Wall. Steppe-traversing horses, not ocean-traversing sailing ships, were the sovereign means of locomotion by which the separate civilizations of the world as it was before A.D. 1500 were linked together—to the slight extent to which they did maintain contact with each other.

In that world Babur's Farghana was the central point, and the Turks were, in Babur's day, the central family of nations. A Turcocentric history of the world has been published in our lifetime by the latest in the series of great Ottoman Turkish Westernizers, President Mustafa Kemal Ataturk. It was a brilliant device for restoring the morale of his fellow-countrymen, but it was a still more brilliant feat of genuine historical intuition; for from the fourth century of the Christian era, when they pushed the last of their Indo-European-speaking predecessors off the Steppe, down to the seventeenth century, which witnessed the collapse of the Ottoman, Safawi, and the Timurid Turkish dynasties in their respective domains of Rum, Iran and India, the Turkish-speaking peoples really were the keystones of the Asiatic arch from which the pre-da Gama belt of civilizations hung suspended. During these 1200 years, the overland link between the separate civilizations was commanded by Turkish steppe-power, and from their central position in this pre-da Gaman world, the Turks rode out conquering and to conquer, east and west and south and north: to Manchuria and Algeria, to the Ukraine and the Deccan.

But now we come to the great revolution: a technological revolution by which the West made its fortune, got the better of all other living civilizations, and forcibly united them into a single society of worldwide range. The revolutionary Western invention was the substitution of the Ocean for the Steppe as the principal medium of world-communication. This use of the Ocean, first by sailing ships and then by steamships, enabled the West to unify the whole inhabited and habitable world, including the Americas. Babur's Farghana had been the central point of a world united by horse-traffic over the Steppe; but in Babur's lifetime the centre of the world made a big jump: . . . the steppe-ports were put out of action when the ocean-going sailing-ships superseded the camel and the horse.

X / THE MUSLIM CLIMATE OF THOUGHT

INTRODUCTION

The most striking feature of the intellectual history of the century 1450-1550 is that during this period the West at last caught up with and overtook Islam, though the latter was quite unaware of what was happening. The Renaissance had no effect whatever on the Muslim world. The Muslims remained unshakably convinced of the superiority of their culture, as they had been for centuries among the pioneers in the advance of human knowledge. Now this leadership was being challenged and undermined by the revival of Greek philosophy and learning and the growth of experimental science in the West, but of this Islam knew and cared nothing. The development of thought and science in Islam had already been checked by the wars and invasions of the Turkish-Mongol age, which ruined so many old centers of learning, and by a rising distrust of profane knowledge on the part of the powerful *ulama,* the doctors of the Sacred Law, the accepted guardians of orthodoxy and of the purity of the faith. To the theologians of Islam, the only study that mattered was that which helped to a deeper knowledge of God and understanding of religion: All else was frivolous and superficial, if not downright dangerous. Arabic philosophy, which had borrowed a good deal from ancient Greek thought, came to be denounced as atheistic and had been effectively suppressed as early as 1200. The study of the natural sciences was pursued with some success for a longer time, but was in rapid decline by 1500, at a time when the West was on the eve of its biggest advance in this field. Thus the Copernican theory of the earth's motion round the sun, which revolutionized cosmological thinking in Europe, was ignored in Islam: The breakdown in intellectual communication between the two civilizations was now almost complete. The humanities in Islam suffered less; the writing of history, for example, never ceased, and the historians of Mogul India, who wrote in Persian, reached a high standard. But the old Arabic learning, long centered in Cairo, was dealt a severe blow by the Ottoman conquest of Egypt in 1517. Many scholars migrated to Constantinople, and those who remained could no longer count on the patronage of an independent Egyptian government. The rise of the Safavids in Persia had a chilling effect on the arts and sciences alike: A narrow puritan theocracy had no use for such things, and many of the ablest Persian artists and scholars moved to India and entered the service of the Moguls. In the Ottoman Empire art and letters did indeed flourish; this was a golden age of Turkish poetry and historiography, but there was nothing whatever comparable to the scientific movement in the West, and the printing-press was scorned as an infidel novelty and not used in the Sultan's dominions to print Muslim books till 1727. Islam had become a self-contained civilization, which felt no further need of taking anything from outside: Its exponents had no doubt that it possessed all truth.

37 / A PIOUS MUSLIM SCHOLAR "REFUTES" PHILOSOPHY AND SCIENCE

One of the most strikingly original of Muslim thinkers was the great Tunisian Ibn Khaldun (A.D. 1337-1406), whose chief work was a History of the Berbers, to which he prefixed an elaborate introduction called the Muqaddimah. In this he surveyed the whole field of human knowledge as it was known to him and worked out—virtually the first to do so—a most impressive philosophy of history. Yet notwithstanding his ardent quest for truth, this devout and deeply religious Muslim was darkly suspicious of philosophy proper, which he thought weakened theological faith, and of those branches of the natural sciences that served no practical or utilitarian end. The pursuit of profane knowledge seemed to him unbecoming in a true Muslim, it wasted time that would be much better spent in the cultivation of religious learning, and at worst it might lead to the shipwreck of a man's faith in God, His Prophet, and His Law. Ibn Khaldun probably spoke for the vast majority of his educated coreligionists, both in his own day and in succeeding generations. The study of history was permissible and even laudable, because it showed the working out of God's relations with His people, and was necessary for the elucidation of the Koran, the life of the Prophet, and the early caliphs. This is why the writing of history continued even in the worst periods of Islamic decadence.

It may be noted that Ibn Khaldun's views attracted the attention of Ottoman scholars, and a Turkish translation of his book appeared in 1730.

The following extracts from the Muqaddimah *illustrate the author's distrust of and contempt for most nontheological learning and help us to understand why the Renaissance passed Islam by. No Muslim of that age would have considered for a moment that he had anything to learn from pagan Greeks and Romans, who lived centuries before the revelation of God to Muhammad.*

The intellectual sciences are natural to man, inasmuch as he is a thinking being. They are not restricted to any particular religious group. They are studied by people of all religious groups who are equally qualified to learn them and to do research in them. They have existed (and been known) to the human species since civilization had its beginnings in the world. They are called the sciences of philosophy and wisdom. They comprise four distinct sciences.

1. The first science is logic. It is a science of protecting the mind from error in the process of evolving unknown facts one wants to know from the available facts. Its use enables the student to distinguish right from wrong wherever he so desires in his study of the essential and accidental perceptions and apperceptions. Thus, he will be able to ascertain the truth concerning created things, within the limits of his ability to think.

2. Then, philosophers may study the elemental substances perceivable by the senses, namely, the minerals, the plants and the animals which are created from the elemental substances, the heavenly bodies, natural motions, and the soul from which the motions originate, and other things. This discipline is called "physics." It is the second of the intellectual sciences.

From *The Muqaddimah: an Introduction to History* by Ibn Khaldun. From trans. by F. Rosenthal, vol. 3, pp. 111-12, 116-18, 153-55, 246-53. Copyright © 1958 by Routledge & Kegan Paul Ltd. London. Reprinted with permission of the publisher and Bollingen Foundation.

3. Or they may study metaphysical, spiritual matters. This science is called "metaphysics." It is the third of the intellectual sciences.

4. The fourth science is the study of quantities [measurements]. It comprises four different sciences, which are called the "mathematical sciences."

The first mathematical science is geometry. It is the study of quantities [measurements] in general. The second is arithmetic. The third is music. The fourth is astronomy. These are the basic philosophical sciences. . . .

The intellectual sciences and their representatives succeeded to some degree in penetrating Islam. They seduced many people who were eager to study those sciences and accept the opinions expressed in them. In this respect the sin falls upon the person who commits it. "If God had wanted it, they would not have done it."

We hear now that the philosophical sciences are greatly cultivated in the land of Rome [Western Europe] and along the adjacent northern shores of the country of the European Christians. They are said to be studied there again and to be taught in numerous classes. Existing systematic expositions of them are said to be comprehensive, the people who know them numerous, and the students of them very many. God knows better what exists there. . . .

Recent speculative theologians confused the problems of theology with those of philosophy, because the investigations of theology and philosophy go in the same direction, and the subject and problems of theology are similar to the subject and problems of metaphysics. . . . It seemed as if the purpose which the theology and philosophy followed in their respective subjects and problems was one and the same.

This confused people, but it is not correct. The problems with which the science of speculative theology deals are articles of faith derived from the religious law as transmitted by the early Muslims. They have no reference to the intellect and do not depend on it in the sense that they could not be established except through it. The intellect has nothing to do with the religious law and its views. Speculative theologians do not use the [rational] arguments they talk about as do the philosophers, in order to investigate the truth of the [articles of faith], to prove the truth of what had previously not been known, and to make it known. [Their use of rational arguments] merely expresses a desire to have rational arguments with which to bolster the articles of faith and the opinions of the early Muslims concerning them, and to refute the doubts of innovators who believe that their perceptions of [the articles of faith in their interpretation] are rational ones. [Rational arguments were used only] after the correctness of the articles of faith, as they had been received and believed in by the early Muslims, had been stipulated by traditional evidence.

There is a great difference between the two positions. The perceptions which the Master of the religious law [Muhammad] had are wider [than those of the philosophers], because they go beyond rational views. They are above them and include them, because they draw their support from the divine light. Thus, they do not fall into the canon of weak speculation and circumscribed perceptions. When the Lawgiver [Muhammad] guides us towards some perception, we must prefer that perception to our own perceptions. We must have more confidence in it than in them. We must not seek to prove its correctness rationally, even if [rational intelligence] contradicts it. We must believe and know what we have been commanded to believe and know. We must be silent with regard to things of this sort that we do not understand. We must leave them to the Lawgiver [Muhammad] and keep the intellect out of it.

The only thing that caused the theologians to use rational arguments was the discussions of heretics who opposed the early Muslim articles of faith with speculative innovations. Thus, they had to refute these heretics with the same kind of arguments. . . . The argumentation of the theologians thus came to look as though it were inaugurating a search for faith through rational evidence. This is not so. Speculative theology merely wants to refute heretics. The things it investigates are stipulated by the religious law and known to be true. . . . God is the guide to that which is correct.

The harm they [the sciences] can do to religion is great. Therefore, it is necessary that we make clear what they are about and that we reveal what the right attitude concerning them should be.

There are certain intelligent representatives of the human species who think that the essences and conditions of the whole of existence, both the part of it perceivable by the senses and that beyond sensual perception, as well as the reasons and causes of these essences and conditions, can be perceived by mental speculation and intellectual reasoning. They may also think that the articles of faith are established as correct through intellectual speculation and not through tradition, because they belong among the intellectual perceptions. Such people are called "philosophers," which is Greek and means "lovers of wisdom."

It should be known that the sciences customarily known among civilized people are of two kinds. There are the sciences which are wanted *per se,* such as the religious sciences of Koranic interpretation, Prophetic tradition, jurisprudence and speculative theology, and the physical and metaphysical sciences of philosophy.

Scholars whom God led astray adopted their doctrines and defended them. . . . It should be noted that the opinion the philosophers hold is wrong in all its aspects. . . . The problems of physics are of no importance for us in our religious affairs. . . . Therefore, we must leave them alone.

The great philosopher Plato said that no certainty can be achieved with regard to the Divine, and one can state about the Divine only what is most suitable and proper—that is, conjectures. If, after all the toil and trouble, we find only conjectures, the conjectures we had at the beginning may as well suffice us. What use, then, do these sciences and the pursuit of them have? We want certainty about the *existentia* that are beyond sensual perception, while in their philosophy, those conjectures are the limit that human thinking can reach.

38 / THE DECLINE OF MUSLIM CULTURE

While higher education in the West was expanding to include Greek science and philosophy, and the new art of printing was multiplying books to an extent never before known, the method and content of instruction in Islam remained unchanged and books continued to be laboriously copied by hand down to the eighteenth century and even later. Yet Muslim devotion to learning remained strong, and in countries like Indonesia and West Africa where Islam was spreading in this age, the mosques that were built became places of instruction as well as of worship. Emphasis was always placed, however, on the teaching of the Koran, the hadith (*or traditions*), *and the Law;*

the ulama, strongly conservative, distrusted secular learning, which in consequence received little encouragement or endowment. Gibb and Bowen's Islamic Society and the West, *from which the following extract is taken, is concerned principally with Ottoman social conditions in the eighteenth century, but the analysis by these two scholars of the Turkish educational system applies equally well to an earlier age.*

It is important to appreciate the narrowly vocational and technical character of the training given at el-Azhar [the great Muslim "university" in Cairo] and all similar institutions. Neither teacher nor pupil regarded it as anything other than the acquisition of a certain amount of "knowledge," all such knowledge being a known or knowable quantity with strictly defined boundaries. To overstep these boundaries, or to question them in any way, was to incur the suspicion and disapprobation of one's fellow "knowers," or in certain cases even the penalty of expulsion from their corporation and loss of livelihood, as well as of reputation. The inevitable result of such a system, over which no quickening breath had blown since the beginning of the sixteenth century, was to intensify both the narrowness of the educational range itself and its narrowing effect on the minds of the educated. The biographies of shaikhs and scholars include lengthy lists of books and pamphlets which show no decline in quantity from the literary output of earlier centuries, but even within the fields of study most cultivated—those of law and theology—it is doubtful if more than a fraction preserved a trace of the ancient quality. If the dead-point of a society is reached when the educational forces are no longer effective to influence or direct its development, it must be admitted that the dead-point was long since passed in Islamic society. Education had ceased to set before itself even the hope of moulding society in the directions of its ideals, and had sunk to the level of merely holding society together by the inculcation of tradition.

Yet there remains something to be set upon the other side. Making all allowances for the defects of the hereditary system and the rule of thumb of vocational training, there is still to be seen, among

From *Islamic Society and the West* by Gibb and Bowen, vol. 1, part ii, pp. 159-61. Copyright © 1957 by the Oxford University Press, London. Published under the auspices of the Royal Institute of International Affairs. Reprinted with permission of the Oxford University Press.

a substantial proportion of the learned, a genuine zeal and devotion to learning. The typical Muslim *'alim* (scholar) remains a student to the end of his days, and whether he travels to Cairo, Mecca or Istanbul, or remains at home, he always seeks out the most noted scholars and attends their lectures. The travelling shaikh receives a warm welcome from his brethren, and is sure of a lodging either in their houses or in a *madrasa*. Thus continuity of contact is ensured, and a strong sense of solidarity maintained among the *Ulema*, which makes for keeping up the professional standard. While some of their intellectual activities may have been misdirected and their initiative stifled by the cramped sphere in which they moved, the historian must recognize that it was due to them and to the work of the religious brotherhoods that the civilization of Islam did not founder in the cataclysms of the later medieval centuries. Seen in this light, even their narrowness and unyielding grip of tradition becomes understandable and justified, since their task was indeed to hold society together in a period of confusion and economic decline, when it could not afford to take the risk of intellectual adventure.

While the social function of education must therefore be given full recognition, its intellectual quality must finally be judged by the character of its products. In this connexion, however, it would be unjustifiable to criticize the "medievalism" of the Islamic world in itself; in its isolation from the rest of the civilized world, and lacking any but the most superficial contact with Western Europe (and that only in Istanbul), it inevitably retained all those medieval characteristics which were then being overcome but slowly even in the West. Amongst these was the belief in astrology and divination, of which numerous examples could be given, and the closely-allied occult literature, divided into some half-dozen "sciences." The popular and thaumaturgical practices of Sufism powerfully aided the spread of occultism, with such success as practically to silence all criticism and opposition. Many shaikhs were indeed highly esteemed for their skill in amulets and charms, not only by the vulgar but also by the learned.

The real gravamen of the criticism to be brought against Islamic intellectual culture is that it had fallen so far below even its own medieval standards and appeared to be quite unconscious of the decline.

GLOSSARY

Amir (emir)—commander, prince, general.

Arquebus—early type of portable gun.

Barud—gunpowder.

Bastinado—corporal punishment by caning soles of feet.

Bektashis—monastic order of dervishes.

Bey (beg)—lord, chief.

Beylerbey—governor of an Ottoman province.

Cadi (qadi, kadi, kazi)—judge.

Capadan—captain, governor.

Comerchieri—customs official.

Dervish (darwish)—member of a religious fraternity.

Devshirme—periodical levy of Christian boys for Ottoman government service.

Dhimmis—literally "protected people." Christians and Jews living under Muslim rule.

Divan (diwan)—council, government department.

Fakir—holy man.

Fetwa (fatwa)—religious decree.

Franks—Muslim name for all West Europeans.

Ghazi—hero, fighter for the faith.

Haj—pilgrimage. Haji (hajji)—one who has made the Mecca pilgrimage.

Imam—leader.

Janissaries—corps d'élite of the Ottoman Army. (Turkish Yeni Cheri-"new troops").

Jihad—holy war.

Jinn (genie)—supernatural beings.

Ka'ba—the sacred temple at Mecca.

Kanun—Ottoman law.

Khutba (khotba)—mosque sermon.

Lak (lac)—100,000 rupees.

Madrasa (medresa)—school.

Maidan—open space where military exercises are performed.

Mamluk (Mameluke)—white slave, as distinct from *abd,* a black slave.

Marj—meadow; often found in place-names, e.g. Marj Dabik: "Dabik Meadow."

Matchlock—a musket having a match for lighting the powder.

Millet—a religious community in the Ottoman Empire having its own chiefs and laws.

Mir—shortened Persian form of the Arabic *amir* (q.v.).

Mirza—title given to the family and descendants of Timur or Tamerlane, later applied generally like "esquire" in England.

Moors—common European name for non-Turkish Muslims in the sixteenth and seventeenth centuries.

Mufti—jurist, adviser on the sacred law.

Muslim (Moslem)—one who professes the faith of Islam. A Persian form of the name is *Musulman.*

Pasha—lord, chief.

Reis—captain.

Rum (Roum)—Asia Minor, formerly part of the *Roman* or Byzantine Empire.

Sanjak—standard, banner, province, administrative district.

Shaikh al-Islam—head of the *ulama* (q.v.).

Shari'a (Sheri)—sacred law of Islam.

Shi'a (Shiah)—the "party" of Ali.

Sophi—European name for the Persian ruler of the *Safavid* dynasty (A.D. 1500-1722).

Tekke—Bektashi convent.

Timar—non-hereditary fief in the Ottoman Empire.

Tugh—crest or pennant of horse-tails. "Pashas of three tails" were those of the highest rank.

Ulama (ulema)—religious chiefs, doctors of the canon law.

Voivode—Slavonic title meaning commander, governor, or prince.

Zamorin—Hindu ruler of Calicut, in South India.

THE MUSLIM ERA

The Muslim calendar dates from July 16, A.D. 622, the year of Muhammad's flight or withdrawal (hijra, hegira) from Mecca to Medina. The Muslim year, being a lunar one of 354 days, is steadily catching up to the Christian year.

Unless the Hijra *month* be known, it is often impossible to say in which Christian year an event should be placed. Thus the Hijra year 906 began on July 28, A.D. 1500, and ended on July 16, A.D. 1501, so we are obliged to say A.H. 906 = A.D. 1500-1501.

See W. Haig, *Comparative Tables of Muhammadan and Christian Dates* (London, 1932), or the *Handbook of Oriental History*, ed. C. H. Philips (London, 1951), which give the Muslim equivalents of Christian era dates up to A.D. 2000.

A NOTE ON MUSLIM NAMES

Muslim names often appear in two or three forms: Arabic, Persian, or Turkish.

In the Arabic alphabet, unlike the Persian and Turkish, there is no *ch, e, o,* or *p.* Thus the name of the Persian town *Ispahan* is transliterated *Isfahan* in Arabic, and while the Persians call China *Chin,* the Arabs call it *Sin.*

The Prophet's name is *Muhammad* in Arabic, but in Turkish is pronounced *Mehmet, Mehmed,* or *Mehemet.* From the latter is derived the incorrect European form, *Mahomet.*

A Muslim's name commonly consists of: 1. a personal name, which is either (a) a slightly disguised form of a well-known Biblical name, e.g., Ayub (Job), Harun (Aaron), Ibrahim (Abraham), Musa (Moses), Sulaiman (Solomon), Yakub (Jacob), and Yusuf (Joseph); or (b) a compound made up of Abd ("slave") followed by Allah ("God"), or one of the so-called "Ninety-nine Divine titles," e.g., Abd al-Aziz ("Slave of the Mighty");

2. the *kunya,* usually compounded with Abu ("father"), e.g., Abu Musa Ali—"Ali, father of Musa";

3. the *nasab,* or pedigree, introduced by ibn ("son"), e.g., Ibn Khaldun, "Khaldun's son";

4. the *lakab,* or descriptive epithet or nickname, e.g., al-Rashid, "the right-guided";

5. the *hisba,* an adjective derived from place of birth or residence or trade, e.g., Omar Khayyám, "Omar the Tentmaker."

CHRONOLOGY

1453	Ottoman Turks take Constantinople.
1479	Turks take Kaffa in the Crimea and gain control of the Black Sea.
1480	Turks take Otranto in south Italy. Russians under Ivan III check advance of Golden Horde on Moscow.
1481	Death of Muhammad (Mehmet) the Conqueror. Bayezid II Sultan.
1482-95	Prince Jem, Bayezid's brother, held hostage by the Christian Powers.
1492	Granada, last Muslim outpost in Spain, falls to the Christians. Columbus sails to the discovery of the New World.
1493	Muhammad Ture becomes *askia* (ruler) of Negro Muslim kingdom of Songhai.
1498	Portuguese under Vasco da Gama reach Calicut.
1500	Shah Isma'il inaugurates Shi'ite regime in Persia. Shabani, khan of the Uzbeks, drives Babur from Samarkand.
1502	Destruction of the Golden Horde.
1503	Ludovico di Varthema becomes the first European to enter Mecca and Medina.
1509	Portuguese defeat Egyptian-Mamluk fleet off Diu.
1510	Shabani defeated and killed by Shah Isma'il.
1511	Portuguese take Malacca.
1512	Sultan Bayezid deposed by his son Selim the Grim. Massacre of Shi'ites in Asia Minor.
1513	Portuguese repulsed from Aden.
1514	Battle of Chaldiran—Sultan Selim defeats forces of Shah Isma'il.
1516	Sultan Selim overthrows Mamluks at Marj Dabik in Syria.
1517	Egypt annexed to the Ottoman Empire.

1519   Khair ad-Din Barbarossa confirmed by Sultan Selim as Governor of Algiers.

1520   Death of Sultan Selim. Sulaiman the Magnificent Sultan.

1522   Turks take Rhodes; Knights of St. John migrate to Malta.

1524   Death of Shah Isma'il.

1525   Babur invades India.

1526   Battle of Panipat—beginning of Mogul empire in India. Battle of Mohacs—Ottoman Turks conquer Hungary.

1527   Ahmad Gran from Somaliland attacks Abyssinia.

1529   Ottoman Turks besiege Vienna.

1538   Turco-Egyptian fleet routed by Portuguese off Diu.

1541-43   Portuguese help Abyssinians to drive out the Muslim invaders.

1553   Last Ottoman naval incursion under Piri Reis into the Indian Ocean.

PRINCIPAL MUSLIM SOVEREIGNS

Ottoman Sultans	A.D.	A.H.
Muhammad (Mehmet) II, the Conqueror	1451-81	855-85
Bayezid II, the Saint	1481-1512	885-918
Selim I, the Grim	1512-20	918-27
Sulaiman II, the Magnificent	1520-66	927-74
Safavid Shahs		
Isma'il	1500-24	906-31
Tahmasp I	1524-76	931-84
Mamluk Sultans		
Kansuh al-Ghuri	1501-16	907-22
Tuman Bey	1516-17	922-23
Great Moguls		
Babur	1525-30	931-37
Humayun	1530-56	937-63
Akbar	1556-1605	963-1014

BIBLIOGRAPHY

No general history of the Muslim world in this age exists: only regional studies are available.

The literature on sixteenth-century Turkey is fuller than on other contemporary Islamic lands, but even so there is no satisfactory history of the Ottoman Empire in English. A useful sketch is W. S. Vucinich, *The Ottoman Empire: its Record and Legacy* (Princeton, 1964: Anvil Series), and reference may be made to L. S. Stavrianos, *The Balkans since 1453* (New York, 1958). A. H. Lybyer's *Government of the Ottoman Empire in the Time of Suleiman the Magnificent* (Cambridge, Mass., 1913) is not yet outdated, and remains the fullest analysis of Turkish institutions. Bernard Lewis's *Istanbul and the Civilization of the Ottoman Empire* (Norman, Okla., 1963) is a penetrating essay, and W. H. Allen's *Problems of Turkish Power in the Sixteenth Century* (London, 1963) a brief but stimulating survey of the Empire in its international setting.

Of biographies of the Sultans, the finest is Franz Babinger's *Mehmed der Eroberer* (München, 1953), a thorough, scholarly study of the conqueror of Constantinople, which has been translated into French and Italian but not yet into English. Barnette Miller's *Palace School of Muhammad the Conqueror* (Cambridge, Mass., 1941) describes the system of training for Ottoman public service as it developed in the reign. On Bayezid II, see V. J. Parry's article in the new *Encyclopaedia of Islam,* and his chapter, "The Ottoman Empire 1481-1520," in the *New Cambridge Modern History,* I (1957), and S. N. Fisher's *Foreign Relations of Turkey 1481-1512* (Urbana, Ill., 1948); on his brother Jem, see L. Thuasne's *Djem-Sultan* (Paris, 1892). There is nothing recent on Selim I, but the long reign of his famous successor is well covered in R. B. Merriman's *Suleiman the Magnificent* (Cambridge, Mass., 1944).

A mass of information on religious conditions in Turkey is contained in F. W. Hasluck's *Christianity and Islam under the Sultans* (2 vols., Oxford,

1929). J. K. Birge's *The Bektashi Order of Dervishes* (London, 1937) is a valuable monograph on the most influential of Ottoman religious fraternities.

Little is available in English on Persia. Shah Isma'il still awaits a Western biographer. The best account of the rise of the Safavids is in E. G. Browne's classic *Literary History of Persia,* Vols. III and IV (Cambridge, Eng., 1920, 1924). Sir Percy Sykes's *History of Persia* (2 vols., London, 1930) is a rather uninspiring compilation.

For Mamluk Egypt, see Sir William Muir's *The Mameluke or Slave Dynasty of Egypt* (London, 1896) and Stanley Lane-Poole's *History of Egypt in the Middle Ages* (London, 1901; 4th ed.: 1925), both somewhat old-fashioned in treatment. An excellent though restricted recent study is D. Ayalon's *Gunpowder and Firearms in the Mamluk Kingdom* (London, 1956).

On Mogul India, see the *Cambridge History of India,* vol. 4, "The Mughal Period" (Cambridge, Eng., 1937). The volume on "The Delhi Sultanate" in the *History and Culture of the Indian People* series (Bombay, 1960) is the most recent account of India on the eve of Babur's invasions. Stanley Lane-Poole's *Babar* (London, 1899), in the "Rulers of India" series, is the best short biography. Babur's own autobiography has been translated and annotated by Mrs. A. S. Beveridge as *The Babur-nama in English* (2 vols., London, 1922).

The spread of Islam in Malaya and Indonesia is well described in D. G. E. Hall's *History of South East Asia* (London, 1954) and Sir Thomas Arnold's *The Preaching of Islam* (London, 1896). For the Golden Horde and the Uzbeks, see R. Grousset's *L'Empire des Steppes* (Paris, 1939; 4th ed.: 1952) and G. Vernadsky's *Russia at the Dawn of the Modern Age* (New Haven, 1959).

The best book on Muslim Negro Africa is E. W. Bovill's *Golden Trade of the Moors* (Oxford, 1958). An English version of Leo Africanus is included in the Hakluyt Society series, *The History and Description of Africa* (3 vols., London, 1896): the new French translation, *Description de l'Afrique* (2 vols., Paris, 1956) is preferable.

The struggle between Christendom and Islam in Europe, in the Mediterranean and the Indian Ocean may be studied in Dorothy Vaughan's *Europe and the Turk* (Liverpool, 1954), a most useful pioneering work. The fullest account of the naval wars in the Mediterranean is F. Braudel's *La Méditerranée et le Monde méditerranéen à l'époque de Philippe II* (Paris, 1949), a masterpiece of erudition dealing though with the late rather than the early sixteenth century. Stanley Lane-Poole's *Barbary Corsairs* (London, 1890) is now largely outmoded, and supplanted by Sir

Godfrey Fisher's *Barbary Legend* (London, 1957), which strongly defends the Muslim States of North Africa against the charge of being notorious for piracy and misgovernment. For the Portuguese in the Indian Ocean, see R. S. Whiteway's *Rise of the Portuguese Power in India* (Westminster, 1899), a little out of date, but still useful; R. B. Serjeant's *The Portuguese off the South Arabian Coasts* (Oxford, 1963), well documented from Arabic sources; and J. S. Trimingham's *Islam in Ethiopia* (London, 1952), for the Christian-Muslim conflict in Abyssinia.

On the intellectual life of Islam, see R. A. Nicholson's *Literary History of the Arabs* (Cambridge, Eng., 1907), and E. G. Browne's *Literary History of Persia,* especially vol. IV (Cambridge, Eng., 1924). A good sketch of Turkish literature is given in the first volume of E. J. W. Gibb's *History of Ottoman Poetry* (London, 1900). Ibn Khaldun's *Muqaddamah* (Eng. tr.: 3 vols., London, 1958), though written in the fourteenth century, accurately reflects the Muslim mind during the next few generations. Adnan Adivar's *La Science chez les Turcs ottomans* (Paris, 1939) is a most interesting attempt by a Turkish scholar to defend Islam against the charge of scientific backwardness and to claim connections between Turkey and Renaissance Europe. Gibb and Bowen's *Islamic Society and the West* (2 parts, Oxford, 1950-57), though primarily concerned with Turkish social life and conditions in the eighteenth century, has a great deal that is relevant to earlier times. See also J. J. Saunders, "The Problem of Islamic Decadence," *Journal of World History,* VII (1963), 701-720; T. Stoianovich, "Factors in the Decline of Ottoman Society in the Balkans," *Slavic Review,* XXI (Dec. 1962), 623-32; and B. Lewis, "Some Reflections on the Decline of the Ottoman Empire," *Studia Islamica,* IX (1958), 111-127.